CHRISTOLOGY IN THE NEW TESTAMENT

General Editors
Core Biblical Studies
Louis Stulman, *Old Testament*
Warren Carter, *New Testament*

Other Books in the Core Biblical Studies Series
The Apocrypha by David A. deSilva
The Dead Sea Scrolls by Peter Flint
Apocalyptic Literature in the New Testament by Greg Carey
God in the New Testament by Warren Carter

CORE BIBLICAL STUDIES

CHRISTOLOGY IN THE NEW TESTAMENT

DAVID L. BARTLETT

Abingdon Press
Nashville

CHRISTOLOGY IN THE NEW TESTAMENT
Copyright © 2017 by Abingdon Press

All rights reserved.

No part of this work may be reproduced or transmitted in any form or by any means, electronic or mechanical, including photocopying and recording, or by any information storage or retrieval system, except as may be expressly permitted by the 1976 Copyright Act or in writing from the publisher. Requests for permission should be addressed in writing to Permissions, Abingdon Press, 2222 Rosa L. Parks Blvd., PO Box 280988, Nashville, TN 37228-0988, or e-mailed to permissions@abingdonpress.com.

Library of Congress Cataloging-in-Publication Data has been requested.

ISBN: 978-1-4267-6635-0

Unless otherwise indicated, all scripture quotations are from the Common English Bible. Copyright © 2011 by the Common English Bible. All rights reserved. Used by permission. www.CommonEnglishBible.com.

Scripture marked NRSV is from the New Revised Standard Version of the Bible, copyright 1989, Division of Christian Education of the National Council of the Churches of Christ in the United States of America. Used by permission. All rights reserved.

Scripture marked RSV is from the Revised Standard Version of the Bible, copyright 1952 [2nd edition, 1971] by the Division of Christian Education of the National Council of the Churches of Christ in the United States of America. Used by permission. All rights reserved.

Scripture quotations marked KJV are from The Authorized (King James) Version. Rights in the Authorized Version in the United Kingdom are vested in the Crown. Reproduced by permission of the Crown's patentee, Cambridge University Press.

Greek Bible text from: Novum Testamentum Graece, 27th revised edition, Edited by Barbara Aland and others, © 2001 Deutsche Bibelgesellschaft, Stuttgart.

Scripture marked AT is from the author's own translation.

To Carol, Benjamin, Jonah, and Elizabeth
"Now faith, hope, and love abide."

Contents

Acknowledgments ix
General Preface xi

Chapter 1
Jesus of Nazareth 1

Chapter 2
Jesus's Resurrection: The Turning Point 13

Chapter 3
Titles for Jesus 23

Chapter 4
The Beginning of the Gospel(s) 39

Chapter 5
Singing about Jesus: Hymns and Prayers in the New Testament 57

Chapter 6
Practical Christology: Paul and His Letters 79

Chapter 7
Stories Jesus Tells 97

Chapter 8
Stories about Jesus: The Gospels (Mark and Matthew) 119

Chapter 9
Stories about Jesus: The Gospels (Luke and John) 143

Notes 161
Scripture Index 167

Acknowledgments

On behalf of Abingdon Press, Warren Carter and David Teel invited me to write this book. I am grateful for the invitation and for David's help with the logistics of the project. Warren has been an exemplary editor, and I'm grateful for his guidance.

Much of the content of the book began as material for classes on Christology for graduate programs at Columbia Theological Seminary and at the Seminario Evangelico de Teologia in Matanzas, Cuba. My understanding of the material was greatly enriched by the interaction with students in those classes.

Chapter 4 grew out of the "Trinity Explores" programs at Trinity Presbyterian Church in Atlanta. I was privileged to serve as theologian in residence at that church for four years and will be forever grateful for their partnership in the gospel.

Tom Jones, a friend from Trinity, read the manuscript and made invaluable suggestions.

I am deeply grateful to my colleagues at Columbia Theological Seminary and at Yale Divinity School for their friendship and their wisdom. All of them contribute to my continuing education. Several have made particular suggestions for this book: Harold Attridge, Adela Yarbro Collins, Michal Beth Dinkler, Mark Douglas, and Raj Nadella. I thank you all.

This book has been richly informed by fifty years of conversations on Christology with George Stroup. Our students will be glad to know that sometimes we talk about other things too.

Acknowledgments

As I worked on this book I realized how much of my adult life I had spent working through questions of interpretation set by Norman Perrin. Years ago, he was my senior colleague at the University of Chicago for a very brief year before his sudden death. He was uniquely self-assured and argumentative. I never got the chance to thank him.

General Preface

This book, part of the Core Biblical Studies series, is designed as a starting point for New Testament study.

The volumes that constitute this series function as gateways. They provide entry points into the topics, methods, and contexts that are central to New Testament studies. They open up these areas for inquiry and understanding.

In addition, they are guidebooks for the resulting journey. Each book seeks to introduce its readers to key concepts and information that assist readers in the process of making meaning of New Testament texts. The series takes very seriously the importance of these New Testament texts, recognizing that they have played and continue to play a vital role in the life of faith communities and indeed in the larger society. Accordingly, the series recognizes that important writings need to be understood and wrestled with, and that the task of meaning making is complicated. These volumes seek to be worthy guides for these efforts.

The volumes also map pathways. Previous readers in various contexts and circumstances have created numerous pathways for engaging the New Testament texts. Pathways are methods or sets of questions or perspectives that highlight dimensions of the texts. Some methods focus on the worlds behind the texts, the contexts from which they emerge, and especially the circumstances of the faith communities to which they were addressed. Other methods focus on the text itself and the world that the text constructs. And some methods are especially oriented to the locations and interests of readers, the circumstances and commitments that readers bring to the text in interacting with it. The books in this series cannot engage every dimension of the complex mean-making task, but they can lead readers along some of these pathways. And they can point to newer pathways that encourage further explorations relevant to this cultural moment. This difficult and complex task of interpretation is always an unfolding path as readers in different contexts and with diverse concerns and questions interact with the New Testament texts.

A series that can be a gateway, provide a guide, and map pathways provides important resources for readers of the New Testament. This is what these volumes seek to accomplish.

Warren Carter
General Editor, New Testament
Core Biblical Studies

Chapter 1
Jesus of Nazareth

New Testament Christology is the study of what the writers of the New Testament claimed about the story and the significance of Jesus of Nazareth. From the very first days of the Christian movement believers asserted that Jesus was not only an identifiable, historical human being but also the unique representation of God. Different writers expressed that uniqueness in different ways, but all of the New Testament writers believe something like what Matthew asserts. Jesus is *Emmanuel*, which means "God with us" (Matt 1:23).

The first line of the earliest Gospel, Mark, says that Mark's book is about the good news of Jesus, who is also Christ, or Messiah (Mark 1:1). In the earliest writings in the New Testament the Apostle Paul almost always refers to Jesus as "Jesus Christ" or "Christ Jesus." For the New Testament writers, there was no way to talk about Jesus without also acknowledging that he was Christ or Messiah.

However, in more recent studies of the New Testament a number of scholars—those who believe that Jesus is God's unique representation and those who think that he was simply an admirable historical figure—have tried to ask what we can say about Jesus that everyone could agree on.

Because we live in the twenty-first century it may be useful to start with a twenty-first-century question: what can we say about Jesus of Nazareth before we study the claim that he is also Messiah or Christ?

"How Do We Look for Jesus?"

New Testament Christology is the study of what the first Christian writers believed about Jesus Christ. Though we tend to think of *Jesus Christ* as the full name of Jesus, the English version of the name of the man who is the subject of Christology is *Jesus*. *Christ* is the English transliteration of the Greek word *Christos,* which is a translation of the Hebrew word *Messiach,* which means "anointed one." *Jesus* is a name; *Christ* is a title. The elementary school child who thought that the first president of the United States was named General Washington confused a title with a name.

It is unclear whether Jesus thought of himself as the Messiah or whether the claim that he was the Messiah and the use of the title *Christ* first was the work of those who followed him. For some centuries now a number of scholars and writers have tried to discover or to imagine who Jesus was and whether or not he thought of himself as the Messiah.

One way to look at this search for who Jesus was is to say that scholars have been trying to find out what pretty much everyone can agree about when it comes to Jesus. Whether or not you believe that Jesus was the Messiah, whether or not you believe that he was son of God, whether or not you are a Christian, what can you say about him? The attempt is to try to reconstruct Jesus's life from our sources just as someone might want to reconstruct the life of Julius Caesar or William Shakespeare or Sojourner Truth.

This attempt to discover what we can know about Jesus apart from faith in him, this attempt to treat him like any other historical person is usually called "the quest of the historical Jesus."[1]

It turns out that drawing a portrait of Jesus that everyone can agree is accurate is largely impossible. (This is also true of Julius Caesar, William Shakespeare, and Sojourner Truth, so we should not be surprised.)

Partly this is because the sources we have about Jesus were written some time (several decades) after his life, and for Jesus, as for everybody, time tends to reshape memories. Partly this is because the sources we have do not all agree on some elements of Jesus's life. Partly this is because the earliest sources we have were all written by people who *did* believe that Jesus was the Messiah. They were not simply describing him; they were trying to persuade others to join them in that belief. The last verse of the twentieth chapter of the Gospel of John actually works well to summarize the writings of all four Gospel writers and the letters in the New Testament too: "But these things are written so that you will believe that Jesus is the [Messiah], God's Son, and that believing, you will have life in his name" (John 20:31).

The final complication is perhaps the most complicating of all. Those who seek to portray Jesus often portray him in ways that they find especially congenial or especially relevant to their own time. Albert Schweitzer, who was a great organist and a medical missionary in addition to being a brilliant student of the New Testament, noticed at the beginning of the twentieth century that the people who had written about the historical Jesus in the few centuries before always ended up portraying just the Jesus they wanted. To put it too simply, German scholars portrayed an orderly Jesus, French scholars a passionate Jesus, English scholars a polite Jesus.[2] As for Americans, to this day there is considerable literature that suggests that the real Jesus was an entrepreneur—the perfect model for capitalist success. One fairly recent book is simply titled: *Jesus, CEO*.[3]

When we try to draw a picture of Jesus that everyone could agree on—believers and nonbelievers alike—there are at least three approaches. Each has some value.

The first approach, one that is essential and inescapable, is to try to get some sense of the world in which Jesus lived. He was born, taught, and died in an eastern province of the Roman Empire. Like many other people of his time and place he was a Jew, but Judaism in the first-century CE was not exactly like Judaism today, and we need to discover as much as we can about first-century Judaism, especially in Palestine.

He was also the inhabitant of an empire and finally was subject to the rule of Rome. Roman emperors were the final authorities in the empire of the first century, but local decisions were usually made by local officials, and many of those officials were recruited from the inhabitants of the territory. There were different customs in different parts of the empire; and in order to understand Jesus, it helps to understand something of what that empire was like and especially how Rome related to the province where Jesus lived.

The empire was also remarkably diverse; it embraced a number of religions, and its subjects spoke a number of languages. While Jesus, like many of his fellow Palestinians, probably spoke Aramaic—a kind of cousin to Hebrew—much of the most influential literature of the time was written in Greek or Latin, and much of the written business of the time was conducted in Greek. Paul, who is the earliest writer in the New Testament, wrote his letters in Greek, and the four Gospel writers all wrote in Greek. While I am not very confident about trying to reconstruct Aramaic teachings of Jesus behind our Greek texts, it helps to remember that he taught in a language different than the language of our New Testament.

The second approach to drawing a picture of Jesus is to concentrate on the teachings we have, especially in Mark, Matthew, and Luke. In this approach the attempt is not to discover everything that Jesus may have said—that is beyond even the most ambitious search. The attempt is to discover, among the things that Jesus is supposed to have said, what sayings were almost certainly original.

This approach was perhaps best exemplified by my late colleague Norman Perrin who wrote a highly influential book called *Rediscovering the Teaching of Jesus*.[4] Perrin had a number of sophisticated ways of trying to winnow our Gospels in order to retain (rediscover) what Jesus really said. The heart of his argument was that we can be most certain that a saying comes from Jesus if it does not simply seem like a repetition of the Jewish teachings he would have inherited or like an invention of the early church put back in Jesus's mouth by later believers. (The stories about Jesus were passed on by word of mouth for a long while before they were written down, and some of the sayings may have been expanded in the telling. Furthermore, Christians believed that Jesus was still alive and probably still speaking. For a first-century Christian to say "Jesus said" doesn't necessarily mean that the Christian believed that Jesus had said it in Galilee during his ministry there.)

This concern for "dissimilarity"—for finding sayings that don't seem to repeat the tradition before Jesus or mirror the traditions after Jesus—has been one of the main inspirations for the Jesus Seminar, founded by Robert Funk and others and still alive and well in our day.[5]

To take just one example on which many scholars would agree, at the end of the Gospel According to Matthew, Jesus tells his disciples to go throughout the whole world baptizing "in the name of the Father and of the Son and of the Holy Spirit" (Matt 28:19). That sounds to many like a quotation of the words early Christians would have used to baptize new members—words that are well on the way to the later doctrine of the Trinity. To many readers of the New Testament (and to me), it seems more likely that some early Christians took a saying that was part of their own worship services and put it directly into the mouth of Jesus.

The attempt to rediscover Jesus by looking for what is unique in his teaching raises problems, however. For one thing, as almost all of these scholars would admit, when you get what is indisputably what Jesus said, you don't begin to get the full Jesus. What you get (as they admit) are the red passages in the edition of the New Testament published by the Jesus Seminar—the bare minimum on which they all can agree.

For another thing, as a teacher of mine long ago pointed out, pushed to its radical conclusion, this kind of quest for Jesus would be satisfied only with sentences that were largely incomprehensible. We couldn't explain them by the context from which they arose or by the implications that they had for the later life of believers. All language is rooted in the past and opens to the future.

Bearing these cautions in mind, I am still enough a student of Perrin to try with great tentativeness and some humility to guess what Jesus almost certainly said—not as the end but as the beginning of the larger quest for what he *probably* said.

The third approach is perhaps best represented by E. P. Sanders and Dale Allison Jr.[6] In somewhat different ways and with somewhat different conclusions they want to ask about continuities and probabilities in what Jesus said and did. Sanders is especially concerned to say that we can understand Jesus in part by reading the stories about his actions, not just by a recitation of his sayings. In particular, suggests Sanders, Jesus's activity in stirring up a ruckus in the Jerusalem temple shortly before his arrest helps us understand why he was arrested and helps us understand what kind of teaching might have led up to that memorable behavior.

Allison is particularly concerned to find continuities in the stories about Jesus. What motifs occur time and again? What events or teachings might account for later developments in the church? Granting that coherence is often in the eyes of the student, Allison does a remarkable job of trying to discover in the diverse sources a kind of plausible picture.

Our own attempt to describe Jesus in terms that might be persuasive both to believers and unbelievers depends on all three of these approaches. In presenting this portrait I admit that it is necessarily tentative and inescapably shaped by perspectives that I bring to the task and often do not recognize even in myself. In presenting this portrait I also say what I will say again. The life, the teachings, the ministry, and the death of Jesus of Nazareth (Jesus without the "Christ") provide one way of beginning to understand Christology—but only a beginning. The development of Christology will require the faith of Jesus's followers.

What Do We Find?

The first irrefutable fact about Jesus is that he was a Jew. We remember this not only as a protection against the implicit and explicit forms of anti-Judaism that have appeared from the first century to the twenty-first. We remember that Jesus was a Jew because apart from that fact his ministry and his teachings are incomprehensible.

The presupposition with which Jesus lived his life was that the God of Israel was the one God of all the world. Jesus was theistic without apology and monotheistic without reservation. Many of the arguments that contemporary people want to have (Is there a God? Is the universe created or accidental? Why worship? Are there immutable religious and ethical principles?) are simply never argued in Jesus's teaching, because the answers are assumed in the way any religious first-century Jew would assume them: there is one God, the creator who establishes immutable principles including the principle that we are to worship that God.

Jesus's scripture was what we call either the Old Testament or the Hebrew Bible. When he argued he drew his conclusions from scripture, and when he told stories he drew his images from scripture. I suspect that one reason the Apostle Paul seems to have instructed Gentile converts in the Old Testament is that they would not have been able to make any sense of Jesus without it.

It is clear that Jesus saw himself as a reformer of the Judaism of his day. It is possible that he began to envision a message that extended to Gentiles, too; certainly by very early after his death, Jewish followers were commending him to curious Gentiles. What seems unlikely is that he saw himself as the founder of a religious community in competition with the temple or with the synagogue. What seems likely is that like the prophets before him and like many a Jew after him, he wanted to purify the faith in which he lived.

When we ask what we can say with some certainty about the events of his life, the odd rule still seems useful. If the story is embarrassing but still remembered and retold, that is probably because it is an inescapable part of Jesus's story. It is what everybody knew.

(This is different from Norman Perrin's criterion of "dissimilarity," which counts a saying as genuine if it does not sound too much like what Jews were saying before Jesus's ministry or too much like what the church was saying afterward.)

The biggest embarrassment and the most irrefutable feature of Jesus's story is that Jesus was crucified. Whatever hopes his followers may have had for him, those hopes could not have included the hope that he would be executed as a criminal—perhaps as a political prisoner. Whatever made it so hard for Saul of Tarsus (the Apostle Paul) to believe that this man was who his followers said he was, was the fact that Jesus was crucified. What at first seemed to Saul/Paul most outrageous turned out to be most inspiring, but none of that takes away from the sheer fact that this man was executed.

The New Testament sources know, but do not much emphasize, that Jesus would only have been crucified because he was sentenced by the Roman authorities. Execution by crucifixion was a punishment inflicted by the imperial authority, not by the provincial Jewish leaders and not by the officers of the temple. We do not know precisely what charges were brought against Jesus, but it seems likely that something more than blasphemy was involved. Who he was and what he did threatened the realm and not only the faith.

I am largely persuaded by E. P. Sanders that what precipitated Jesus's arrest was the incident in the Jerusalem temple early in the week of his arrest, and perhaps along with this the so-called triumphal entry into the city. Whatever Jesus intended, the actions in the temple could be interpreted as the beginnings of insurrection, and the march into the city could be interpreted as an unsettling political demonstration.

In large measure the development of Christology—the subject of the rest of this book—was an attempt to explain how Jesus the Christ could also be the crucified one. But we should not lose sight of the reality that that execution took some explaining.

A second embarrassing feature of the story about Jesus is that he was baptized by John the Baptizer. In the first century of the Common Era, John the Baptizer is better known by non-Christian writers than Jesus is.[7] John was what we would call an "apocalyptic" preacher; he believed that the present age was passing way and that God was about to establish God's own rule. According to the New Testament stories, John baptized people when they repented of their sins. A less theological reading might suggest that John baptized people who chose to be his followers.

Whether John baptized to acknowledge repentance or baptized in order to welcome followers, it was something of a problem for the earliest Christians that Jesus got baptized by John. We can see in all four Gospels the ways in which the Gospel writers try to explain this. The explanation always includes the fact that John the Baptist is inferior to Jesus.

This embarrassment leads to one inevitable conclusion and to one possible one. The inevitable conclusion is that Jesus was baptized by John sometime before Jesus began his own public ministry. The likely—but by no means certain—conclusion is that Jesus began his adulthood as a follower of John's (the one who baptized him) and only later broke away. The Gospel of John in particular suggests that some of Jesus's first disciples had been followers of John the Baptizer first. For whatever reason, Jesus broke away and began his own alternative movement (see John 1:35-37).

I also agree with Dale Allison (and Albert Schweitzer) that it seems as certain as any such theory can be that Jesus began his ministry as an "apocalyptic" preacher. Like John the Baptizer he sees the end of the present age and expects the coming reign of God in glory and in judgment.

It is hard to understand how the early Christian movement could have been so thoroughly immersed in that kind of end-time expectation without thinking that some of the expectation goes back to Jesus himself. In different ways the writer of Luke and Acts and the writer of John's Gospel try to revise the early expectations to explain why the kingdom is taking so long to arrive in its fullness, or to find another way of talking about judgment altogether. But it seems plausible that they were moving away from a tradition that expected judgment soon. What does not seem plausible is that Jesus had an entirely different way of viewing the world and that the (not much) later New Testament writers spent so much effort affirming or correcting this apocalyptic thinking although it had no original relation to him whatsoever.

Our reading of the evidence is that Jesus had an "apocalyptic" belief in the coming of God's reign on earth—quite soon.

It is not clear whether Jesus taught that he himself would be the agent of that coming kingdom. The three "synoptic" Gospel writers—Mark, Matthew, and Luke—give us many sayings to that effect, and a quick look at 1 Corinthians 15 will show us that Paul thought the same. It seems plausible that in the light of their belief that Jesus was the Christ (and in light of their belief in his resurrection, about which more soon) early Christians came to believe that the Christ who preached the coming kingdom would also herald its arrival in person, though Jesus himself had not made such a claim. It is also entirely possible that Jesus declared himself as agent of the coming age.

It is almost certainly true that Jesus believed that the kingdom of God was not to come but that it had already begun, especially in his ministry. When he casts out a demon he explains his action by saying: "If I throw out demons by the power of God, then God's kingdom has already overtaken you" (Luke 11:20). Parables like the story of the mustard seed (the little seed that grows into the great tree from Mark 4:30-32) and the seed growing secretly (Mark 4:26-29) suggest that Jesus believed that the kingdom to come had already begun. Mark says that Jesus began his ministry by saying something like: "The time is fulfilled and the Kingdom of God has one foot in the door" (Mark 1:15 AT). Whether or not Jesus said exactly that, it is a good summary of much of his teaching.

The fact that Jesus says that his casting out of demons is a sign of the kingdom may prove an embarrassment to us, but it was hardly an embarrassment to his first hearers or to the first readers of the New Testament. They took for granted that there were spirits in the world acting in opposition to the Spirit of God. It seems overwhelmingly likely that Jesus shared this perception and that he acted upon it. As far as we can tell, Jesus's first critics never argued that he did not perform extraordinary works; they argued that he did so by working for the demonic forces themselves.[8] Nor was Jesus unique as an exorcist. In Mark's Gospel his supporters acknowledge that others cast out demons (Mark 9:38).

In the light of his own preaching about the kingdom that is breaking in, Jesus claims for himself the right to be an interpreter of the law. It is impossible to know how much of the Sermon on the Mount goes back to Jesus himself, but certainly chapter 6 of Matthew and a number of Jesus's disputes with his opponents suggest that he saw himself as a true interpreter of the Torah. Like Moses, only more so.

In our section on stories in chapter 7 we shall see some of the ways in which the Gospels have Jesus interpret the law. We can guess that the stress on breaking down some of the divisions between insiders and outsiders and the claim that the law was as much humanity's servant as it was its master may go back to Jesus himself.

Once you grant that much of the New Testament was written after some decades of reflection on Jesus's life, and if you are not convinced that the New Testament is invariably factually accurate, you are bound to admit that it is very hard to know exactly what Jesus claimed of himself. Did he call himself Messiah? Son of Man? Son of God? The answer to those questions seems unknowable. What is knowable is what the early Christians said about him.

Why was he believed to be not only Jesus but also Jesus Christ? To that question we now turn.

For Further Reading

Allison, Dale C., Jr. *Constructing Jesus*. Grand Rapids: Baker Academic, 2010.

Crossan, Dominic, et al. *The Jesus Controversy*. Harrisburg: Trinity Press International, 1999.

Keck, Leander. *Who Is Jesus?* Edinburgh: T&T Clark, 2001.

Perrin, Norman. *Rediscovering the Teaching of Jesus*. New York: Harper and Row, 1978.

Sanders, E. P. *The Historical Figure of Jesus*. London: Penguin, 1993.

Schweitzer, Albert. *The Quest for the Historical Jesus*. Translated by John Bowden et al. Minneapolis: Fortress Press, 2001.

Sobrino, Jon. *Christology at the Crossroads: A Latin American Approach*. Translated by John Drury. Maryknoll: Orbis, 2002.

Chapter 2

Jesus's Resurrection: The Turning Point

In our first chapter we tried to discover what a historian could tell us about Jesus, without raising the question of Jesus's significance for believers and for communities of faith. In this chapter we will look at the ways in which Jesus's followers from at least the time of his resurrection appearances made claims about his unique significance for believers and indeed for the whole world.

It is difficult if not impossible to decide whether "the historical" Jesus claimed to be Messiah, Son of God, or Lord. What is quite clear is that in the very earliest days after his death, his followers began to use all of these titles for him. What led the earliest Christians to use these titles for Jesus, or what confirmed their use of these titles, was their belief in his resurrection from the dead. The resurrection was the turning point after which believers would claim that Jesus was God's unique representative on earth.

The main reason early believers began to call Jesus *Messiah* and *Son of God* and *Lord* was that they knew and believed the stories of his resurrection. Without faith in Jesus's resurrection from the dead it is likely that he would have been remembered only as Jesus and not celebrated as Jesus Christ. Or he would not have been remembered at all.

The claim that Jesus rose from the dead is not as easy to understand as it might seem, and it is impossible to prove.[1]

One difficulty arises from the fact that the accounts of Jesus's resurrection differ from one New Testament writer to another. Another difficulty arises from the fact that many twenty-first-century people are convinced by all kinds of evidence that death is irreversible; the claim that Christ died and rose again seems literally incredible.

A third difficulty is that the New Testament claims about Jesus's resurrection are not just claims about a man being dead and then being alive again. We have one story like that in the account of Lazarus in John 11 and another story like that in the account of Jesus's raising the son of the widow of Nain in Luke 7. Those are both fascinating stories, but the claims about Jesus's resurrection go far beyond the claim that he got out of the tomb.

For early Christians, Jesus's resurrection is the proof of God's victory over death—for Jesus first and then for all believers, or perhaps for all creation. Jesus's resurrection is the vindication of the claim that Jesus is not just a revivified Jew but Israel's Messiah. Jesus's resurrection is, by some accounts, the great act that made him Son of God. Jesus's resurrection is the first act in the long drama by which God will establish God's rule over all the cosmos. Jesus's resurrection is the beginning of his continued presence among believers. He is both a living guide to the faithful and the living object of right worship.

No list of historical witnesses and no citation of scientific probabilities can give us all that. But the people who first told the stories believed all that—so the stories were told not as proofs but as testimonies. From the first day until now the claim that Christ is risen is a claim of faith about God's power as well as a claim about what happened outside Jerusalem long ago. So, too, the claim that Jesus is the Christ is finally not simply a description. The claim that Jesus is the Christ is an act of faith. What strengthened and perhaps even initiated that faith was the resurrection.

The Appearances of the Risen Jesus

The earliest account we have of the resurrection of Jesus comes from 1 Corinthians. Paul is writing quite soon after Jesus's death (probably in the 50s of the Common Era). Furthermore, he is quoting an account that he himself heard, probably when he first became a believer. So these sentences represent a very early account of Jesus's rising from the dead:

> I passed on to you as most important what I also received: Christ died for our sins in line with the scriptures, he was buried, and he rose on the third day in line with the scriptures. He appeared to Cephas, then to the Twelve, and then he appeared to more than five hundred brothers and sisters at once—most of them are still alive to this day though some have died. Then he appeared to James, then to all the apostles. (1 Cor 15:3-7)

That seems to conclude the account that Paul received and is passing on. He then adds his own autobiographical note: "Last of all he appeared to me, as if I were born at the wrong time" (1 Cor 15:8).

Note several features of this account. First, the risen one is not named *Jesus* but simply *Christ*, so very early in the tradition the identification of Jesus and Messiah is virtually assumed. To say *Christ/Messiah* is to name Jesus. Second, the resurrection of Jesus is inescapably bound together with his crucifixion; for the earliest Christian tradition, death and resurrection are the central events that identify Jesus as Messiah and are inseparable each other. Third, the events Paul narrates take place "in line with the scriptures." For early Christians the scriptures (our Hebrew Bible or Old Testament) were the revelation of the will and plan of God, so to say that something happened in line with the scriptures is to say that it was part of God's deliberate plan.[2] All this is to say that Paul cannot even recite the tradition without making a number of claims based in faith; he cannot tell Jesus's story without acknowledging Jesus as Christ. Fourth, the appearances of the risen Jesus are not restricted to the period just after the resurrection (forty days in Luke and Acts), for years later Jesus appears to Paul. It may be that Paul thinks the appearance to him is the last appearance; at least it makes him the last of the apostles.

Of course this is not a historical description of what happened at the resurrection. However, Paul does indicate a couple of features of the event. First, it happened "on the third day." Some twentieth- and twenty-first-century theologians want to say that the resurrection event occurred only gradually. Some believe resurrection took place as believers remembered Jesus's importance and value: the memory was the resurrection. Some believe resurrection took place as Christians—like Paul—began to preach resurrection. Christ rose into the preaching of the church: the proclamation was the resurrection. Some believe that Christ rose into the experience of believers—the sense of Christ's presence in worship and prayer was written back into the narrative of his life. What was really an ongoing, almost mystical experience was retold as if it were a distinct historical event: the religious experience was the resurrection.

While there is no question that for the earliest Christians resurrection was evident in memory, in preaching, and in religious experience, there is also no question that for Paul and the tradition before him resurrection was an event; it was datable. It happened on the third day.

And resurrection was confirmed by appearances of the risen Messiah. At various points in the New Testament (here, Mark 16:7; John 21) it seems that Jesus's resurrection appearance was especially linked to the testimony of Peter; and it may be the case that Peter's prominence in the early church came not just from his relationship to Jesus in Galilee but to his claim to have seen the risen Lord.

However, Paul also wants to insist that the resurrection appearances were not confined to the circle of those who had known the earthly Jesus and were not confined to the first days after the crucifixion. Paul, too, has seen the risen Christ. We have accounts of this encounter between Paul and the risen Christ not only here but also in Galatians 1:11-16 and Acts 9:1-22, 22:4-16, and 26:9-18. When Paul says of Jesus's appearance to him that Christ appeared "last of all" he might mean simply that this is the end of the list and that Paul does not expect Jesus's appearances to continue now that Paul himself has been validated as an apostle—as a witness to the risen Lord.

The Empty Tomb

It is not at all clear whether Paul knew the story that the risen Jesus left behind an empty tomb. When a Corinthian Christian heard the claim that Paul had received that "he was buried, and he rose on the third day" does that imply that in rising Jesus was unburied—that he left behind an empty tomb (1 Cor 15:4)?

In any case, along with the tradition of Jesus's resurrection appearances—starting with his appearance to Peter—there is another group of stories about Jesus's resurrection that concentrate first on the empty tomb and that stress the importance, not of Peter, but of Mary Magdalene and other women followers of Jesus.

The earliest of the four Gospels—the four accounts of Jesus's ministry, death, and resurrection—in the New Testament is almost certainly the Gospel according to Mark. In writing their accounts Matthew and Luke rely very heavily on Mark's Gospel.

Mark's account of Jesus's resurrection is found in Mark 16:1-8:

> When the Sabbath was over, Mary Magdalene, Mary the mother of James, and Salome bought spices so that they might go and anoint Jesus' dead body. Very early on the first day of the week, just after sunrise, they came to the tomb. They were saying to each other, "Who's going to roll the stone away from the entrance for us?" When they looked up, they saw that the stone had been rolled away. (And it was a very large stone!) Going into the tomb, they saw a young man in a white robe seated on the right side; and they were startled. But he said to them, "Don't be alarmed! You are looking for Jesus of Nazareth, who was crucified. He has been raised. He isn't here. Look, here's the place where they laid him. Go, tell his disciples, especially Peter, that he is going ahead of you into Galilee. You will see him there, just as he told you." Overcome with terror and dread, they fled from the tomb. They said nothing to anyone, because they were afraid.[3]

This seems an odd ending to readers who know the other three Gospels or who have read the passage from 1 Corinthians 15 that we have just discussed. While the young man promises the women that they will see the risen Jesus, Jesus does not appear to them in this Gospel. Perhaps that seems strange to us only because we have read the other accounts. Perhaps the author of this Gospel ended it just as he wanted to: with an empty tomb and a promise.

The ending is further complicated, however, by the fact that in the Greek text Mark's Gospel seems to end in mid-sentence. There is no very good way to translate his Greek into our English, but it is a bit as if the last word, not just of a sentence, but of a whole story was *because*. The writing tutor would send the writing student home to try again.

In any case, we note three features of this earliest Gospel tradition:

First, what is at most implicit in Paul is explicit here. As of the third day after the resurrection, Jesus's body was not in the tomb.

Second, this important discovery is closely associated with Jesus's women followers. Paul almost certainly includes women among the larger crowds who saw the risen Jesus, but he does not name any particular female witnesses to the resurrection. And Mark seems to recognize the special place of Peter when it comes to the resurrection because the women are to tell Peter first what they have seen and then, along with him, the other disciples.

Third, while the risen Jesus does not appear to anyone within the verses of this Gospel the young man promises that Jesus, the risen one, will appear; this confirms the promise that Jesus himself makes in Mark 14:28, and there is no question in Mark's Gospel that Jesus is a faithful commentator on his own story.

Matthew's Gospel (in chapter 28) follows Mark quite closely up to the point where the women arrive at the tomb. Then Matthew makes clear that the absence of the stone from the tomb is a miracle. The young man of Mark's Gospel becomes two angels in Matthew's Gospel (Matthew tends to double the numbers of his minor characters throughout the Gospel). And the risen Jesus really does appear before the story is over. He appears first to the women. Thus Matthew grants them a special place in the resurrection stories, just as Mark had done. Then Jesus appears to make a farewell address to the gathering of the eleven disciples on the mountain in Galilee.

Matthew is unique among the Gospels in his stress on the absolute authenticity of the story of the empty tomb. All this suggests that by the time the Gospel of Matthew is written the story of the empty tomb has spread, and that the response is not that the body was still there but that the body has been stolen. So for Matthew there can be no doubt, resurrection includes the empty tomb, the risen Jesus, and the believing women.

Luke tells his version of the story in chapter 24. Again the women come to the empty tomb, and again they report what they have found to the disciples, but they do not (yet) see the risen Lord. We are led to infer from the quick reference in 24:34 that sometime after this Jesus did appear (first of all) to Simon Peter.

But in the meantime (at the same time? just before? just after? certainly on the third day) Jesus appears to two disciples walking to the village of Emmaus, in a story confined only to Luke's Gospel (see Luke 24:13-35). What is striking about this story is that the two disciples do not recognize the risen Lord until he has interpreted scripture to them and broken bread with them. Surely this reflects the confidence of the early church that Jesus not only lives but also continues to be revealed in the weekly assembly, which would have included preaching (the interpretation of scripture) and communion or Lord's supper or Eucharist—all names for the breaking of the bread.

All this is to underline what we suggested at the beginning of the chapter on resurrection: from the beginning resurrection is not only a matter of evidence but also a matter of faith. And from the beginning the belief in resurrection is not only a belief about what happened on the third day after the crucifixion but also about what continues to happen in the lives of believers and in the worship of the believing community.

The Gospel of John was long considered the most theologically self-conscious of the Gospels. In recent decades we have come to see that each Gospel writer raises theological questions and has theological agendas, but it remains true that John is most effusive in sharing his agenda.

Whatever role Mary Magdalene and Thomas may have played in the earliest stories of the empty tomb and the appearances of the risen Lord, it is clear that in John's Gospel they serve as examples and inspiration to late first-century believers in John's own community. Here is a portion of Mary's story:

> Jesus said to [Mary], "Woman, why are you crying? Who are you looking for?"
>
> Thinking he was the gardener, she replied, "Sir, if you have carried him away, tell me where you have put him and I will get him."

> Jesus said to her, "Mary."
> She turned and said to him in Aramaic, "Rabbouni" (which means *Teacher*). (John 20:15-16)

Mary does not recognize Jesus until he calls her by name. She therefore becomes the perfect model of a sheep of Jesus's fold. The Good Shepherd in the parable, the Good Shepherd risen from the dead, can call the sheep by name (see John 10:1-6).

It is when he calls her name that Mary realizes that Christ is risen indeed.

Then apparently, Mary reaches out to touch Jesus, or even to cling to him, because Jesus says to her: "Don't hold on to me, for I haven't yet gone up to my Father. Go to my brothers and sisters and tell them, 'I'm going up to my Father and your Father, to my God and your God" (John 20:17).

When the Gospel writer tells this story it is not quite clear how he understands Jesus's resurrection. It is quite clear that for John, Jesus's resurrection will be completed only when the Son returns to the Father, from whom he came (see John 1:14). Whether the early readers pictured the risen Lord in some kind of intermediate state between his earthly self and his heavenly glory is unclear. What does seem clear is that John wants Mary's faith to grow. She cannot hold onto the Jesus she has known; none of us can hold onto the past as if we found our purpose there. Mary is called to understand and to follow Jesus, not as the wandering rabbi, but as the risen Lord.

The claim that faithful people know Jesus more through hope than through memory is further elaborated in the story John's Gospel tells of Thomas. Now it becomes clear that faithful people know Jesus through what they hear, not through what they see.

In the story of John's Gospel, Thomas is not condemned for his doubting; he is blessed less richly than he might be blessed because he claims he will trust only what he sees. Jesus makes clear that for the readers of John's Gospel faith will have to come not through seeing but through hearing. After showing Thomas his wounded hands and side, Jesus says to him: "Do you believe because you see me? Happy are those who don't see and yet believe" (John 20:29). This Gospel insists that for the generations of

Christians who are to come, though they will not see the risen Lord, they will believe in him on the basis of what they hear—what they hear when they read this very Gospel, for example.

Nonetheless, though Thomas relies too much on the visible evidence of the resurrection for his faith, the faith he proclaims is the strongest declaration of faith by any of the disciples in the Fourth Gospel: "My Lord and my God" (John 20:28). The people who have heard John's Gospel from its first chapter on have known that this Jesus is the revelation of God—perhaps God's own self. But it is only in the light of the resurrection that Thomas can name Jesus aright. John's Gospel rightly recognizes that Christology begins with the faith that Christ is risen from the dead.

Along with the dramatic narratives of Mary Magdalene and Thomas in this Gospel is the lively story of Peter and the beloved disciple racing toward the empty tomb. Peter gets there first, but the beloved disciple enters first and at least begins to believe. The story, finally written down toward the end of the first century CE, probably reflects some tension between Christians who see Peter as their founding father and those who see the beloved disciple as more central to their customs and beliefs. In any case the story suggests that while our Gospel writer wants to stress the role of Mary and the example of Thomas and above all the truthfulness of the beloved disciple, he knows the tradition that Peter is the first witness of the resurrection; and in his own somewhat indirect way he honors that.[4]

All this is to underline what we suggested at the beginning of the chapter on resurrection: from the beginning resurrection is not only a matter of evidence but also a matter of faith. And from the beginning the belief in resurrection is not only a belief about what happened on the third day after the crucifixion, but also a belief about what continues to happen in the lives of believers and in the worship of the believing community.

For Further Reading

Frei, Hans. *The Identity of Jesus Christ.* Philadelphia: Fortress, 1975.

Madigan, Kevin J., and Levenson, Jon L. *Resurrection: The Power of God for Christians and Jews.* New Haven: Yale, 2008.

Niebuhr, Richard R. *Resurrection and Historical Reason.* New York: Scribner's, 1957.

Swinburne, Richard. *The Resurrection of God Incarnate*. Oxford: Clarendon, 2003.

Williams, Rowan. *Resurrection: Interpreting the Easter Gospel*. Cleveland: Pilgrim Press, 2008.

Wright, N. T. *The Resurrection of the Son of God*. Minneapolis: Fortress, 2003.

Chapter 3

Titles for Jesus

We have already suggested that because the New Testament is written after Jesus's death and resurrection and written by people who believe him to be the fullest revealer of God, it is impossible to know what Jesus might have called himself: Messiah? Son? Prophet?

What is clear is that in the light of their resurrection faith the early Christians chose a number of different titles for Jesus. And though it seems likely that believers applied at least some of these titles to him only after his resurrection, it is also clear that from the start of the churches, when believers told his story, they were perfectly happy to apply those titles to Jesus from his birth to his death and beyond death.

We shall look at four such titles: *Christ, Lord, Son of God,* and *Son of Man*.[1]

Christ

It is possible that the earliest Christian statement we have about Jesus's importance is found in Romans. Here is how Paul begins that letter, telling us something of what he believes about himself and even more what he believes about Jesus:

> Paul, a slave of Christ Jesus, called to be an apostle and set apart for God's good news. God promised this good news about his Son ahead of time through his prophets in the holy scriptures. His Son was descended from David. He was publicly identified as God's Son with power [Or, "He was designated as God's son with power" (AT).] through his

resurrection from the dead, which was based on the Spirit of holiness. This Son is Jesus Christ our Lord. (Rom 1:1-4)

Both because of its literary structure and because of its theological claims, many scholars have thought that Paul is here quoting from a hymn or a prayer that was part of the church's life even before he became an apostle.

For Paul himself the claim that Jesus is the Christ, the Messiah, is so much a conviction that only rarely does he use the name of Jesus cited without the addition of "Christ" or "Messiah." So in this passage Paul says that he is "a servant of Jesus Christ" and that the one risen from the dead is "Jesus Christ our Lord."

By the time of the very earliest Christian writing that we have, 1 Thessalonians—probably written twenty or so years after Jesus's crucifixion and resurrection—Paul begins his letter with these words: "From Paul, Silvanus, and Timothy. To the Thessalonians' church that is in God the Father and the Lord Jesus Christ" (1 Thess 1:1). Paul is not arguing that Jesus is the Messiah, the Christ; he simply assumes that identification. (When I say that I write these words during the administration of President Obama, I'm not making a case that Mr. Obama is president; I assume it.) Paul seldom names Jesus without designating him as the Christ (Rom 3:26, 4:24; 1 Cor 11:23 are among the exceptions.) All this indicates that for believers not that long after Jesus's ministry, it was not only believed but also basically assumed that Jesus was the Christ. This is why when the believers are somewhat derisively given a new name by nonbelievers in the book of Acts they are called *Christians* not *Jesusians* (Acts 11:26). It may also explain why the Roman historian Tacitus wrote in the early second century that a new sect had arisen consisting of people who followed someone named *Chrestos* (Annals 15:44).

What we know of the expectation of many Jewish people of Paul's time tells us that the claim that Jesus was Christ or Messiah is the claim that he is "the anointed one" (our English translation of the Greek *Christos* and the Hebrew *Messiach*). The Messiah is anointed as king, just as David was anointed as king in 1 Samuel 16. At the instruction of the Lord, Samuel chooses David from among his brothers: "He was reddish brown, had beautiful eyes, and was good-looking. The LORD said, 'That's the one. Go anoint him.' So Samuel took the horn of oil and anointed him right there in front of his brothers. The LORD's spirit came over David from that point forward" (1 Sam 16:12-13).

The more we learn about Jews of the first century CE the more we realize that different groups of Jews had different hopes for their own future. Certainly for some Jews the hope was that a leader descended from David would come and rule as a just king. For some Jews this new king would demonstrate God's power by rescuing Israel and Judea from the rule of Rome and establishing an independent kingdom. For some Jews, like the community at Qumran, the Messiah would serve as a great teacher or as a religious leader, a priest. Indeed there is evidence that the Jews at Qumran, who lived separately from the cities and from the temple, awaited two messiahs, one teacher and one priest. Some Jews apparently did not have much hope for an earthly kingdom but hoped that God would bring a new heaven and a new earth soon; for some of these the Messiah was to be an agent of that kingdom that was beyond the kingdoms of this world. Other Jews had no expectation of a Messiah at all.

In the hymn that Paul quotes at the beginning of Romans it seems likely that the first part of the hymn implicitly declares that Jesus was the Messiah. Jesus was "descended from David according to the flesh." For Paul and perhaps for the hymn the realm of the flesh was the present world of daily busyness, politics, and power. In that world, and according to the calculations of that world, Jesus meets the criterion for being Messiah: he is descended from David.

It is clear that the first of the four Gospels begins its first chapter by using a title (or two) for Jesus. While Paul assumes that Jesus is Christ/Messiah and virtually uses *Christ* as part of Jesus's name, Mark, the earliest Gospel, wants to make a clear claim about the significance of the word *Christ* as a title, as a designation, as an honor. The first line of the Gospel reads this way: "The beginning of the good news about Jesus Christ [the Messiah]" (Mark 1:1). (Some early manuscripts go on to say "the Son of God" on this more shortly.) Clearly this verse refers to Jesus with the title the Messiah, the Christ.

The center of Mark's Gospel is found in Mark 8. Numerically this is the central chapter of a Gospel of sixteen chapters. Dramatically it becomes the central moment as Jesus's disciples strive and sometimes fail to understand who he is:

> Jesus and his disciples went into the villages of Caesarea Philippi. On the way he asked his disciples, "Who do people say that I am?"
> They told him, "Some say John the Baptist, others Elijah, and still others one of the prophets."
> He asked them, "And what about you? Who do you say that I am?"
> Peter answered, "You are the [Messiah or the] Christ." Jesus ordered them not to tell anyone about him. (Mark 8:27-30)

It is not entirely clear in this case whether Jesus, as Mark tells of him, thinks that Peter's is a sufficient answer. Instead of referring to himself as *Messiah/Christ*, he refers to himself here and often in Mark's Gospel as *the Son of Man*, and in the subsequent narrative Jesus will help his disciples understand what the title *Christ* or *Messiah* means.

From Matthew's perspective, however, Peter's answer is both clear and clearly right: "[Jesus] said, 'And what about you? Who do you say that I am?' Simon Peter said, 'You are the [Messiah or the] Christ, the Son of the living God.' Then Jesus replied, 'Happy are you, Simon son of Jonah, because no human has shown this to you. Rather my Father who is in heaven has shown you" (Matt 16:15-17). It must be added that what makes the answer clearly right is not only Peter's claim that Jesus is Messiah but also the claim that he is Son of God; Jesus reaffirms what he has just affirmed by referring to God as "my Father."

Luke has a slightly different version of the affirmation, in which Peter answers Jesus's question about his identity, "The [Messiah or the] Christ sent from God" (Luke 9:20). John's Gospel portrays Jesus with a variety of titles and uses a variety of metaphors, but at what is probably the end of the earliest version of his Gospel, John also places central emphasis on the term *Christ* or *Messiah*:[2] "Then Jesus did many other miraculous signs in his disciples' presence, signs that aren't recorded in this scroll. But these things are written so that you will believe that Jesus is the Christ, God's Son, and that believing, you will have life in his name" (John 20:30-31).

Though there are some different nuances in the way early Christian writers understand the title, it is clear that a fundamental assumption of every New Testament writer is that Jesus is rightly called *Messiah* or *Christ*.

Lord

The earliest Christian writings we have are the letters of Paul, and Paul refers to Jesus as "Lord" almost as often as he refers to Jesus as "Christ." While the term *Christ* or *Messiah* is sometimes used almost as a part of Jesus's name, when Paul refers to Jesus as "Lord" it is usually clear that *Lord* is used as a title, an identification, and a proclamation.

Two (of many) passages make clear that *Lord* can be an affirmation of Jesus's special identity and role. In 1 Corinthians Paul is writing to the Corinthians about the variety of gifts that the Holy Spirit gives to believers and insists that to identify Jesus as Lord is itself a proof of inspiration: "No one can say, 'Jesus is Lord,' except by the Holy Spirit'" (1 Cor 12:3).

In Philippians Paul urges the Philippian Christians to humble mutual regard for one another and probably quotes a hymn that ends with a very early Christian affirmation. At the consummation of history when God's rule comes in its fullness: "At the name of Jesus everyone in heaven, on earth, and under the earth might bow and every tongue confess that Jesus Christ is Lord, to the glory of God the Father" (Phil 2:11).[3]

In Mark, our earliest Gospel, the term *Lord* is not often used for Jesus, at least not as part of a theological claim. The Greek word *kyrios* can sometimes also mean "master" or, when used in greetings, "Sir," and in Mark's Gospel it is often not clear whether the more complicated term *Lord* is implied when someone uses *kyrios* when speaking of Jesus as Lord or in addressing him as "Sir."

In Mark 12:35-37 Jesus engages in some complicated biblical interpretation:

> While Jesus was teaching in the temple, he said, 'Why do the legal experts say that the Christ [Messiah] is David's son? David himself, inspired by the Holy Spirit, said, The Lord said to my lord, 'Sit at my right side until I turn your enemies into your footstool.' David himself calls him 'Lord,' so how can he be David's son?

In this interpretation of Psalm 110:1 Jesus indicates that he understands himself as the Messiah/Christ. And he also identifies himself with "the Lord" in the first line from the Psalm: "the LORD [the Messiah] says to my master [David], 'Sit right beside me.'" Complicated as the interpretation is, the fundamental affirmation is clear enough: Jesus cannot simply be called Son of David, because he is not David's son, but David's Lord. Jesus is *the* Lord.

We have looked at the story of Thomas in John's Gospel as one of the narratives in which John portrays faith in the risen Lord. At the end of Thomas's story, Thomas makes the confession that is the strongest claim any disciple makes about Jesus in the Fourth Gospel: "My Lord and my God" (John 20:28).

It is also often the case that the use of *Lord* as a confession of faith is more implicit than explicit. Paul can use *Lord* as a part of Jesus's almost official title: "Grace to you and peace from God our Father and the Lord Jesus Christ" (1 Cor 1:3).

The claim that Jesus is Lord meant at least two things in the world of the early church. First, the claim stood in contrast and opposition to the traditional acclamation of the Roman Empire: "Caesar is Lord." Many students of the New Testament have helped us see the growth of the churches in the context of a world dominated by the power of Rome. Scholars particularly interested in the relationship between faith and empire are often characterized as "postcolonial" writers. Many have been influenced by the work of biblical scholars and theologians in the two-thirds world to recognize how much the status of the New Testament writers as colonial subjects of a distant emperor may have influenced their picture of Jesus—and their hope for him. In such a context, to say that "Jesus is Lord" is to say that Jesus is the true emperor. It is a statement of faith but also a statement of resistance. Warren Carter, in his discussion of Matthew's Gospel, for instance, writes:

> "Lord" denotes God's salvific will and authority over heaven and earth and over human existence.... It denotes Jesus' life-giving authority over judgment, disease, death, creation, and the believing community. It would seem that imperial rule and authority are condemned partly because they claim what rightly belongs to God/Jesus, and partly because

they work against the well being God and Jesus' life-giving purposes accomplish.[4]

Second, in continuity with Greek-speaking Jews, Christians could use the word *kyrios* as a translation of the Hebrew term *adonai*—"my Lord." In Exodus 3:14, when Moses asks God for God's name, God responds with the cryptic phrase that the NRSV translates: "I am who I am." In Hebrew God's claim is really just four letters: YHWH. (In English we usually transliterate this as *Yahweh*; for the King James translators it was *Jehovah*.) For Jews this was (and is) the holiest name of God; even to utter it is blasphemous. So when a Jew who is reading aloud comes to the Hebrew word YHWH he or she substitutes for it another Hebrew word, *adonai*—"my Lord"—a term that obviously refers to God but does not blaspheme by naming the holy name.

Further to complicate matters, when Greek-speaking Jews came to translate the Hebrew Bible into Greek, they translated the Hebrew word *adonai* ("my Lord") into the Greek word *kyrios* ("Lord"). So when a Greek-speaking Jew like Paul or the writer of the Fourth Gospel uses the term *kyrios* or *Lord*, he may be translating the holiest name of God's own self.

That is probably what the writer had in mind when he told the story of Thomas's affirmation to the risen Jesus: "My Lord and my God" (John 20:28). It is almost certainly what the hymn that Paul quotes in the second chapter of Philippians is saying. At the end of history Jesus is given "the name which is above every name" as "every tongue proclaims that Jesus the Messiah is Lord"—*kyrios, adonai,* YHWH—the name that is above every name (Phil 2:9, 11).

In both John's Gospel and Paul's hymn we note that it is only after the crucifixion and the resurrection that Thomas or the early Christians can affirm that Jesus is not only Messiah but also identical with the God so great that God's name is finally unspeakable.

Son of God

The confession that Jesus was Son of God was a way of recognizing Jesus's intimate relationship with God and declaring that he was the agent of

God's purposes. In Romans 1:4 and Acts 13:33 the writers seem to declare that Jesus was made—or at the very least acknowledged—Son of God at his resurrection. While it is impossible to reconstruct with confidence the history of Christian faith before the New Testament writers, it does seem likely that for many early Christians at least the claim that Jesus was God's son was a consequence of his resurrection.

Paul writes: "He was designated Son of God in power according to the Holy Spirit through his resurrection from the dead" (Rom 1:4 AT). The realm of the Spirit for Paul is the realm of God's complete rule, for faith and hope and love are the marks of life in that realm. In these verses, whether Paul creates them or quotes them, we get the sense that Jesus not only was acknowledged as Son of God at the resurrection, but also he became Son of God at the resurrection. As we shall see, more often for Paul we get the sense that Jesus was God's son from the beginning of his ministry—or even from before his birth. However, what we get in this formula is the strong hint that the full faith in Jesus as one with God came out of the faith that God has raised him from the dead.

There is the hint of a similar connection between Jesus's resurrection and his designation as Son of God in Acts 13. Paul is preaching in Antioch and quotes Psalm 2:7 to make his claim about Jesus as God's Son: "We proclaim to you the good news. What God promised to our ancestors, he has fulfilled for us, their children, by raising up Jesus. As it was written in the second psalm, *You are my son; today I have become your father*" (Acts 13:32-33).

In Mark's Gospel, it seems as though Jesus was made God's son by a kind of adoption at the time of his baptism: "About that time, Jesus came from Nazareth of Galilee, and John baptized him in the Jordan River. While he was coming up out of the water, Jesus saw heaven splitting open and the Spirit, like a dove, coming down on him. And there was a voice from heaven, 'You are my Son, whom I dearly love; in you I find happiness'" (Mark 1:9-11).

We remember that the first readers of Mark's Gospel will not have known Matthew, Luke, John, or perhaps even Paul. In some of the earliest manuscripts the very title of Mark's Gospel declares that Jesus is not only Messiah but also Son of God (Mark 1:1). The demons, who have supernatural powers of discernment, recognize that Jesus is son of the most high: "[the man possessed by demons] shouting, 'What have you to do with me, Jesus, Son of the Most High God?'" (Mark 5:7). In Mark, the first human being to acknowledge Jesus as God's son is the centurion at the foot of the cross in Mark 15:39; and when we look at the way in which narratives shape beliefs about Jesus we shall see how important this scene is for Mark. The most trustworthy commentator in Mark's Gospel, of course, is God, and God twice declares that Jesus is Son of God:

> Mark 1:11: "And there was a voice from heaven: 'You are my Son, whom I dearly love; in you I find happiness.'"

> Mark 9:7: "Then a cloud overshadowed them, and a voice spoke from the cloud, 'This is my Son, whom I dearly love. Listen to him!'"

The first heavenly announcement that Jesus is God's son comes at the point of Jesus's baptism, when he comes out of the water and the Spirit descends on him. We have suggested that when the voice says, "This is my son," the implication may be that "as of now this is my son; I adopt him." If so, for Mark the claim that Jesus is son of God is not a claim about his eternal preexistence but a claim about his being chosen as God's agent to manifest God's rule.[5]

Paul, who uses the formula about Jesus being designated Son of God at the resurrection in Romans 1, puts much more emphasis on Jesus as God's son—presumably from the beginning—later in that same epistle: "God has done what was impossible for the Law, since it was weak because of selfishness. God condemned sin in the body by sending his own Son to deal with sin in the same body as humans, who are controlled by sin" (Rom 8:3).

The letter to the Galatians is written in part to remind the Galatians that no one—save Jesus—is a child of God by birthright. All are adopted into God's family through faith in Jesus. The claim that believers are adopted children of God seems to depend on the claim that Jesus was

God's "biological" son from the beginning: "You are all God's children through faith in Christ Jesus. All of you who were baptized into Christ have clothed yourselves with Christ.... But when the fullness of the time came, God sent his son, born through a woman, and born under the Law. This was so he could redeem those under the Law so that we could be adopted" (Gal 3:26-27; 4:4-5).

When the writer of John's Gospel wants to speak of Jesus's sonship he draws in part on the story of Abraham almost sacrificing his son Isaac in Genesis 22. What seems clear here is that Jesus is the Son of God from before the beginning of the story: "God so loved the world that he gave his only Son" (John 3:16).

In the later portions of the Gospel Jesus refers to himself as the Son and as the one sent from God (see John 14:13 and 17:1). When the Gospel writer sums up the purpose of the book he writes: "But these things are written so that you will believe that Jesus is the Christ, God's Son, and that believing, you will have life in his name" (20:31) or "that you might come to believe that Jesus is the Christ, the Son of God."[6]

The Epistles of John were probably not written by the author of John's Gospel, but many think they were written later for the same community of believers. By now the favorite designation for Jesus is "the Son": "What we have seen and heard, we also announce it to you so that you can have fellowship with us. Our fellowship is with the Father and with his Son, Jesus Christ" (1 John 1:3); "This is how the love of God is revealed to us: God has sent his only Son into the world so that we can live through him" (1 John 4:9); "Grace, mercy, and peace from God the Father and from Jesus Christ, the Son of the Father, will be ours who live in truth and love" (2 John 1:3).

For Matthew and Luke, as we will see in the next chapter, the claim that Jesus is Son of God is not a claim about his baptism or (only) a claim about his existence with God from all eternity; the claim that Jesus is Son of God is a claim about his begetting and birth. Now the belief in his divine origin is not only theological but also biological. We shall see some of the implications of this claim in the next chapter.

Son of Man

In all four of the New Testament Gospels Jesus refers to himself as "Son of Man." Two features of this claim are noteworthy. First, this designation for Jesus is used in all four Gospels. Second, in every instance it is Jesus who uses the title for himself. No other character in any of the Gospels addresses Jesus as *Son of Man*, nor does the book of Acts or any of the New Testament letters use that term for Jesus. In the book of Revelation, the risen Lord, who appears to the author in a vision, is twice referred to as "one like the Son of Man." In both these cases Revelation is drawing on Daniel 7:13.

Some have thought that all this indicates that *Son of Man* was Jesus's favored term of reference for himself. Here is a title that does not depend on resurrection faith, but that is part of the teaching of Jesus in the time before his crucifixion. Others have been more skeptical about our ability to trace the title to Jesus's own teaching but see in it another claim that emerged in the early church. In any case the title seems to take on special significance for all four Gospel writers. In all four Jesus is a faithful interpreter of his own mission, and the fact that he refers to himself as Son of Man indicates how central the Gospel writers think the designation is for understanding Jesus's ministry and mission.

Two further observations may help in understanding the function of this term. First, for very good reason, students of the New Testament have wanted to avoid language that seems to stress the fact that the Jesus of history was male and that the glorified Jesus expected at the end of time was to be male as well. This is perhaps especially true when the Gospels are referring to the promise of Daniel 7 that at the end times one "like a Son of Man" will come to establish God's reign. So while the more traditional and more conservative translation of Daniel 7:13 says, "I saw...one like the Son of man [coming] with the clouds of heaven" (KJV) the New Revised Standard Version (NRSV) reads: "I saw one like a human being coming with the clouds of heaven." However, in Mark 13:26, in which Jesus is clearly referring to the passage from Daniel, the NRSV reverts to the more traditional translation: "Then they will see 'the Son of Man coming in clouds' with great power and glory." The Common English Bible

(CEB), an even more recent translation, however, tries to make the phrase more inclusive: "Then they will see the Human One coming in the clouds with great power and splendor."

This is an admirable attempt to try to make a difficult phrase both more understandable and more gender inclusive. However, in order to preserve the continuity between the Hebrew Bible and the New Testament, and in order to preserve the continuity between the Gospels and Hebrews 2:5, we have kept the more traditional translation "Son of Man." Here is how the verse from Hebrews reads: "Now God did not subject the coming world, about which we are speaking, to angels. But someone has testified somewhere, 'What is man that you are mindful of him, Or the son of man that you care for him'" (Heb 2:5-6).[7]

Second, in the early development of Christian faith, at the Council of Chalcedon in 451 CE, the delegates affirmed that Jesus Christ was (and is) "truly God and truly Man" or "truly God and truly human." It is tempting to read this description of Jesus quite narrowly back into the New Testament and to suggest that when Jesus refers to himself as "Son of Man" he is referring to his human status, and when the writers refer to him as the "Son of God" they are affirming his divine status. It is tempting to think that the terms are used to answer a puzzle about the incarnation, a puzzle about the essential personhood of Jesus. We shall see, however, when we look at some of the stories about Jesus, that the New Testament does not have in mind the later development of the doctrine of the two natures and that the phrase *Son of Man* does not refer to the uniquely human features of Jesus. It is a phrase used by him for himself—altogether and all together. And while "Son of God" may sometimes suggest the claim that the Son was with the Father from the beginning, it is also used as a term to claim authority for Jesus in all his words and deeds.

Students of the Gospels have long noticed that when Jesus refers to himself as Son of Man he does so in three kinds of sayings. First, he refers to Daniel's prophecy (7:13) of a figure like a Son of Man who will come at the end of time to help establish God's reign. This is the way the phrase is used in Mark 13:26 and the passages in Luke and Matthew that portray that speech Jesus gives about the end of time. It is also the phrase that

Jesus uses when he makes his own astonishing claim before the high priest in Mark 14:61-62: "Again, the High Priest asked, 'Are you the [Messiah], the Son of the blessed one?' Jesus said, 'I am. And you will see the [Son of Man] sitting on the right side of the Almighty and coming on the heavenly clouds.'"

Notice that in these verses we have three designations for Jesus—Messiah (Christ), Son of God, and Son of Man. These are not three different characteristics or distinct features of his personality but are three different ways of describing the same Jesus. In this particular scene, the Gospel claims that Jesus is the one who establishes God's rule over all things.

Some scholars have thought that the historical Jesus used the quotation from Daniel 7 to refer to a divine figure other than himself who would come at the end of time. According to these authors not long after his death Christian believers began to apply the prophecy to Jesus himself. This is one of those instances of historical guesswork whose accuracy we will probably never know. Certainly in the Gospels, as we have them, the coming Son of Man is Jesus himself.

Second, Jesus uses the phrase *Son of Man* when he predicts his own arrest and death and resurrection. Strikingly in Mark's Gospel where Peter confesses Jesus as the Christ, the Messiah, Jesus neither explicitly accepts nor rejects that designation, but he does go on to present his own self-description: "Then Jesus began to teach his disciples: The [Son of Man] must suffer many things and be rejected by the elders, chief priests, and the legal expers, and be killed, and then, after three days, rise from the dead" (Mark 8:31).

Finally Jesus sometimes uses the phrase *Son of Man* as a kind of substitute for saying *I*. For instance, when Jesus heals the paralytic in Mark 2:1-12, he explains his own miracle: "But so you will know that the [Son of Man] has authority on earth to forgive sins" (v. 10).

In the Gospel of John Jesus refers to himself as "Son of Man" eleven times. He uses the term as a self-designation, but even in the most apparently straightforward texts it seems clear that he designates himself as one with the mission of revealing God. In the story of the man born blind in

John 9, for instance, Jesus comes to meet the blind man after he has been healed and then derided by some of Jesus's opponents:

> Jesus heard they had expelled the man born blind. Finding him, Jesus said, "Do you believe in the [Son of Man]?" [The man formerly blind] answered, "Who is he, sir? I want to believe in him." Jesus said, "You have seen him. In fact, he is the one speaking with you." The man said, "Lord, I believe." And he worshipped Jesus. (John 9:35-38)

At some other points in John's Gospel the title *Son of Man* seems to be particularly linked to the Gospel's stress on a kind of cosmic journey that Jesus undertakes. At the beginning he is with God. He descends to join humankind. He is then raised up in a kind of two-stage return to God. In the first stage he is lifted up toward heaven on the cross; in the final stage, after the resurrection, he completes his journey and returns to the father. In John 3, Nicodemus, a leader of the synagogue, comes to Jesus and they engage in a discussion about Jesus's significance and mission. Jesus says to Nicodemus:

> I assure you that we speak about what we know and testify about what we have seen, but you don't receive our testimony. If I have told you about earthly things and you don't believe, how will you believe if I tell you about heavenly things? No one has gone up to heaven except the one who came down from heaven, the [Son of Man]. Just as Moses lifted up the snake in the wilderness, so must the [Son of Man] be lifted up so that everyone who believes in him will have eternal life. (John 3:11-15)

Here we see in abbreviated form the great journey of the Son of Man, from heaven, to earth, to being lifted up on the cross, and then by implication back to the presence of the Father again.

It seems clear that for all four Gospel writers the title *Son of Man* has a particular association with Jesus and his self-designation. The significance varies from one Gospel writer to another, and it remains a question whether the consistent use of the phrase on Jesus's lips alone indicates an early memory of Jesus's own earthly teaching.

We can never know with confidence exactly what words a first-century reporter or electronic device would have recorded Jesus using to speak about himself. What we do know is that in the light of their faith in his resurrection, the New Testament writers were glad to claim him as Christ/Messiah, as Lord, as Son of God, and perhaps most puzzlingly as Son of Man. Those titles give us some clues as to who the early Christians thought Jesus was. Another set of clues is given to us in the ways that the four Gospel writers begin their narratives about him. That is the subject of our next chapter.

For Further Reading

Carter, Warren. *Matthew and Empire: Initial Explorations.* Harrisburg: Trinity Press International, 2001.

Collins, Adela Yarbro, and John J. Collins. *King and Messiah as Son of God.* Grand Rapids: Eerdmans, 2008.

Hahn, Ferdinand. *The Titles of Jesus in Christology.* Translated by G. Knight and H. Ogg. New York: World, 1969.

O'Collins, Gerald, S.J. *Christology: Origins, Development and Debates.* Waco: Baylor, 2015.

Peppard, Michael. *Son of God in the Ancient World: Divine Sonship in Its Social and Political Context.* New York: Oxford University Press, 2001.

Perrin, Norman. *A Modern Pilgrimage in New Testament Christology.* Philadelphia: Fortress, 1974.

Stroup, George W. *Why Jesus Matters.* Louisville: Westminster John Knox, 2011.

Chapter 4

The Beginning of the Gospel(s)

Each Gospel writer tells us a good deal about his portrait of Jesus by the way in which he begins his Gospel. The earliest Gospel is almost certainly the Gospel of Mark, and then the rest were probably written in the order of Matthew, Luke, and John.

We can see the differences in the way the Gospel writers understand Jesus's significance by noting at what point each of them chooses to begin his story.

For Mark, the story begins with the ministry of Jesus as acknowledged by John the Baptist. Matthew wants to go back further; for him the story begins with the beginning of Jesus's genealogy, his family tree. The story begins with Abraham. For Luke, the story begins with the infant John the Baptist; in chapter 3 Luke gives us the backstory—another genealogy, a somewhat different version of Jesus's family tree. Only now the first ancestor is not Abraham; the first figure in Israel's story, the first ancestor, and the first figure in the story of all humankind is Adam. The story begins with the creation of humankind. In the Gospel of John, the story goes back further yet. Now we do not begin with the creation of humankind (on the sixth day of creation) but even further back to the time before time, to Genesis 1:1, to the very beginning. And now the story of Christ does not begin with the creation of humankind; it begins before the creation of the world.

It would be misleading to suggest that the shift in the time of the beginning of the Gospel represents some kind of self-conscious progress, or the attempt of each Gospel writer to correct his predecessors. It is doubtful that Luke knew what Matthew wrote and unclear whether John knew any of the previous Gospels. Yet the move from the earliest Gospel to the last does represent a shift in the portrayal of who Jesus is, where he comes from, and how he is related to the creator God.

Mark and the Beginning of the Gospel

For those who know the Gospels of Matthew and Luke and for everyone who is familiar with Christmas art—from Hallmark cards to classic nativity paintings—Mark's Gospel seems to start abruptly and late in the story.

Yet almost certainly Mark's was the earliest Gospel, and it is he who first made a judgment about how his story should begin. It is possible that Mark knew the stories of the shepherds now found in Luke's Gospel or of the magi now found in Matthew's, but more likely the story begins with the traditions that had been passed on to him, with the accounts of John the Baptist and of Jesus's own baptism.

Even before he gives us the accounts of John the Baptist and of Jesus's baptism, Mark sets the themes for the book he has written: "The beginning of the good news about Jesus Christ [the Messiah], God's Son" (Mark 1:1).

As far as we know Mark is the first author to write a narrative of Jesus's ministry, death, and empty tomb; and therefore he is the first Christian to hold that this story is gospel, "good news." It seems unlikely that he thought he was writing a new kind of book called "a Gospel." More likely he declares that what the book contains is itself a telling of the good news. Mark is not the first Christian to use the term *gospel*. Writing some years before Mark, Paul uses the term *gospel* often—but for him the good news is primarily the proclamation of Jesus's death and resurrection. It also seems likely that believers before Paul were referring to the good news, but they also meant by that the proclamation of God's love in Jesus—not an account beginning with Jesus's ministry and ending with the empty tomb.

Mark says that the content of this good news is the affirmation that Jesus is "Messiah." Some of our earliest manuscripts add that Jesus is not only "Messiah" but also "Son of God." In chapter 6 we shall see how much the drama of Mark's Gospel leads to the recognition that Jesus is the Son of God, so that whether Mark declares this in the first verse of his work or not, that claim, too, is essential to his good news. In this twofold declaration that Jesus is "the Messiah, the Son of God" (AT), we have at least a hint of the same kind of affirmation we found in Romans 1:3-4 where Paul refers to "the gospel concerning [God's] Son, who was descended from David according to the flesh and was declared [or appointed] to be Son of God with power according to the spirit of holiness by resurrection from the dead" (NRSV). For both Mark and Romans 1, Jesus appears to be Messiah for Israel but Son of God for all of humankind.

If Mark 1:1 is the title for Mark's work there are two ways of reading the claim that this is "the beginning of the good news." It may be that the beginning of the good news refers to the first verses or the first chapter of Mark's work. This is the beginning; then at the end of chapter 1 we move to the middle; and later in Mark, perhaps as Jesus heads to Jerusalem in chapter 10, we move to the end, the conclusion of the Gospel.

The other possibility is that Mark believes that his whole book is "the beginning of the good news"—that what John the Baptist proclaimed and Jesus fulfilled, from baptism to empty tomb—was the beginning of the good news about Jesus that continued to Mark's own day and presumably into the life of the church even after that.[1]

In Mark 1:2-4 Mark moves from his introductory title to show us how the Gospel begins, or how the beginning of the Gospel begins.

As it was written about in the prophecy of Isaiah:

> *Look, I am sending my messenger before you.*
> *He will prepare your way,*[2]
> *a voice shouting in the wilderness:*
>   *"Prepare the way for the Lord;*
>   *make his paths straight."*

John the Baptist was in the wilderness calling for people to be baptized to show that they were changing their hearts and lives and wanted God to forgive their sins.

Even though, unlike the other Gospel writers, Mark does not give a long overture to his presentation of Jesus's ministry, even here we see that the Gospel writer cannot tell the story of Jesus without looking back on what precedes that story.

Part of what precedes that story is John the Baptizer, but even John is not the beginning of the story. What precedes John the Baptizer is the tradition of the Law and the Prophets and here especially the prophecies of Isaiah (joined with Malachi, who is quoted but not acknowledged).

For all the New Testament Gospels, the story of Jesus requires reference to the story of Israel. God has been preparing this good news for a very long time. The idea that we can understand Jesus without understanding the scripture of Israel has no place in our earliest Christian sources.

The tie between Jesus and the history of Israel is further clear in the description of John the Baptist. He dresses and eats like the prophet Elijah. He represents Elijah returned to make Israel ready for the coming Messiah.[3]

It seems likely that when Mark quotes Isaiah, "Look, I am sending my messenger before you," Mark is referring to John the Baptist who has come to prepare the way for Jesus. However, the structure of the paragraph might suggest another interpretation. Usually when a New Testament writer makes a case from the Old Testament by beginning a quotation with the words, "As it is written," the Old Testament verse explains what has just gone before in the passage, not what comes just after.

So in Mark 7:6 after the scribes and the Pharisees have tried to trap Jesus, Jesus cites a quotation that refers back in the text to their actions:

He said to them, "Isaiah prophesied rightly about you hypocrites, as it is written,

> 'This people honors me with their lips,
>   but their hearts are far from me.'" (NRSV; see also Mark 14:27)

If that is the case here also, the quotation from Isaiah and Malachi does not look forward to John the Baptist in verse 3 but back to Jesus in verse 1. Jesus is the messenger who has come to prepare the way of God. If this interpretation is right, we have yet one more description of Jesus who is the hero of this narrative; he is Messiah; he is Son of God; he is God's own messenger.

The narrative of the meeting between John the Baptist and Jesus adds three features to Mark's portrait of who Jesus is.

Jesus Is the Greater One

Here is how Mark portrays John's preaching about Jesus: "One stronger than I am is coming after me. I'm not even worthy to bend over and loosen the strap of his sandals. I baptize you with water, but he will baptize you with the Holy Spirit" (Mark 1:7-8).

In chapter 1 we suggested that while it is difficult to get much clear information about "the historical Jesus"—about what any good historian, believer or not, could discover about Jesus—it seems likely that Jesus began his adult life as a follower of John the Baptist. Therefore it was important for the early Christians to make clear in a variety of ways that Jesus was more important than his former leader. Whether or not Mark remembers any of this, the claim has become an important part of Jesus's story: Jesus is greater than the one who baptized him.

Jesus Inaugurates the New Age

For Mark, as for Paul and many other early Christians, the coming of Jesus Christ marks the shift from the old age of selfishness and sorrow toward the new age of fulfillment and generosity. For Paul, the new age was the new age of the Spirit, as opposed to the old age of the flesh. For Peter, as the book of Acts tells us, the new age was the age when the Spirit was poured out on all people. For Mark, it appears that John's baptism by water was part of the old age; the old age is seen as incomplete. When Jesus comes to be baptized with the Spirit, he inaugurates the new age.

Just after he is baptized, Jesus begins his preaching by saying much the same thing: "Now is the time! Here comes God's kingdom! Change your hearts and lives, and trust this good news!" (Mark 1:14-15). Not only will Jesus baptize with the Spirit, but also, at his own baptism, the Spirit descends upon him. In part this is a mark of God's favor. In part it is the confirmation that the new age of God's reign begins with Jesus. John sets the way; Jesus is the way.

Jesus Is God's Chosen One

While Mark's Gospel tells us that John baptizes people in a baptism of repentance for the forgiveness of sins (1:4), there is no evidence that Mark regards Jesus's baptism in this way. Rather, Jesus's baptism is marked by two signs of his special status. First, as we have noted, the Holy Spirit descends on him as a dove. Whether this means that Mark believed that the Holy Spirit looked like a dove or whether he means that the Holy Spirit descended as a dove descends is not clear. Certainly centuries of Christian art have represented the Spirit as dovelike in shape, not just in motion. In any case the descent of the Spirit marks the shift between the old age of John the Baptist and the prophets and the new age of Jesus, greater than even John and the prophets.

Second, the voice from heaven states, "You are my Son, whom I dearly love; in you I find happiness." The verse echoes Psalm 2:7 where God speaks to the king (a descendant of David):

> *I will announce the Lord's decision:*
> *He said to me, "You are my son,*
> *today I have become your father."*

If Mark knows that this was probably a psalm used at the coronation of the king, then we have here an inauguration in which Jesus is confirmed both as Messiah—heir of David—and as Son of God.

Whereas in Matthew and Luke it is clear that Jesus is born Son of God, in Mark it looks rather more as though he is inaugurated or crowned Son of God at his baptism. What is absolutely clear in Mark's Gospel is that Jesus really is Son of God whether from birth or by adoption. The heavenly voice will make almost the same affirmation in Mark 9:7: "This is my Son, whom I dearly love."

In Mark's Gospel, the voice of God does not make mistakes.

However, we do notice one difference between the declaration in Mark 1 and the declaration in Mark 9. In Mark 1:11 the voice says to Jesus, "You are my Son, whom I dearly love." And it may be the case that at this point in the Gospel, only Jesus hears this good news; only Jesus fully understands his own sonship. In Mark 9:7 the voice speaks to the four disciples who have gone with Jesus to the top of the mountain: "This is my Son, whom I dearly love." During the eight chapters of this Gospel we have moved from a private affirmation to a public announcement. By the end of the Gospel the news will spread far beyond the disciples too.

The Gospel of Matthew

Jesus Is the Fulfillment of God's Plan

The first two chapters of Matthew's Gospel make clear that for Matthew the life and ministry of Jesus are not some kind of divine afterthought. Matthew's Gospel begins with a genealogy that firmly anchors Jesus in the whole story of Israel. Mark 1:1 makes two related claims about Jesus. Both these claims are confirmed in the first chapters of Matthew's Gospel (the "birth narrative") and are further confirmed by the whole Gospel.

First of all, Jesus is Messiah (the word in Greek is *christos,* Christ), and then Matthew expands on that to show that Jesus meets the first requirement for the Messiah, that he is "son of David." However, for Matthew, the story of God's activity in Jesus Christ does not begin just with David. It begins with the beginning of Israel's story, in God's promise to Abraham in Genesis 12:1-3:

> The LORD said to Abram, "'Leave your land, your family, and your father's household for the land that I will show you. I will make of you a great nation and will bless you. I will make your name respected, and you will be a blessing.
>
> *I will bless those who bless you,*
> *those who curse you I will curse;*
> *all the families of the earth*
> *will be blessed because of you."*

Matthew underlines this connection between Jesus and his ancestry by using as the first words of his Gospel "The book of the beginning," which in Greek reads "the book of Genesis" and suggests to people who know the Greek Bible that this is the continuation of the story that begins with Genesis 1:1. (The NRSV translates this phrase not "the book of the beginning/Genesis" but "an account of the genealogy," which is accurate enough but not as suggestive. The CEB's "a record of the ancestors of Jesus Christ" also misses the echo of Genesis.)

The closing of the genealogy suggests that the story of Jesus is the final act in a very well-ordered historical pattern: "So there were fourteen generations from Abraham to David, fourteen generations from David to the exile to Babylon, and fourteen generations from the exile to Babylon to the Christ" (Matt 1:17). All is ordered; all is planned. The way to understand the plan is to read the Law and the Prophets.

We notice that the figure who links Jesus to David and then back to Abraham is Joseph. This connection seems complicated because Matthew will claim very shortly that Jesus's birth fulfilled a prophecy from Isaiah: "Look! A virgin will become pregnant and give birth to a son" (Matt 1:23; see Isa 7:14). In Matthew's Gospel it is very clear that Joseph is not Jesus's biological father.

Joseph, however, takes his rightful place as Jesus's adoptive father. For Matthew, Jesus is born Son of God and adopted Son of David. In two ways Joseph shows that he is Jesus's adopted father. First, he accepts the promise of an angel that the child who will be born to Mary, his fiancée, is not a scandal but a gift from the Holy Spirit. Second, he does what a parent who adopts an infant gets to do: he gives Jesus his name (Matt 1:25).

By implication Joseph gives Jesus his nickname, too. Both the name and the nickname carry special significance. *Jesus* is our English version of the Greek name for Mary's son; our version of the Hebrew name he would have borne is *Joshua*. The name *Joshua* can be interpreted roughly as "the Lord saves." So Jesus's given name means "the Lord Saves." That is why the angel explains the name to Joseph: "You will call him Jesus, because he will save his people from their sins" (Matt 1:21). So from the beginning of his story, Matthew signals that Jesus is who he is because he is one who saves.

The baby's nickname is Emmanuel, "God with us" (Matt 1:23). As we shall see, this name is important to Matthew partly because it fulfills a prediction by the prophet Isaiah. The name is also important because, like the name *Jesus*, it signals something of what Jesus does in Matthew's Gospel: Jesus is "God with us." So in chapter 18 when Matthew is talking about the risen Jesus being present when church people have to discipline a member who goes astray, Jesus says to his disciples and through them to the readers: "For where two or three are gathered in my name, I'm there with them" (Matt 18:20). At the very end of Matthew's Gospel, Jesus again declares his role as Emmanuel—God with us. He promises his disciples and, through them, the church: "Look, I myself will be with you every day until the end of this present age" (Matt 28:20).

Not only does Joseph link Jesus to Abraham and the whole Old Testament story by adopting Jesus, but also Joseph hears and enacts and affirms the prophecies of the Old Testament. When the angel brings Joseph the news that Mary will bear a son, he explains the significance of this moment by quoting from a prophet: "Look! A virgin will become pregnant and give birth to a son, And they will call him, Emmanuel" (Matt 1:23; Isaiah 7: 14).

In the Gospel of Luke and in many of the earliest Christian creeds there is the claim that Jesus was born of the virgin Mary, and Matthew clearly believes this too. But for Matthew the claim is not made so much to suggest that Jesus was conceived by extraordinary means. The main point of the story is that once again, Joseph, Mary, and Jesus fulfill the promises of the Scripture. Like the sets of fourteen generations in the genealogy, this is all part of the plan.

Jesus's Story Retells Israel's Story

Matthew finds yet another way to connect the story of Jesus to the stories of the Old Testament. The term *typology* refers to the way in which an author takes a figure from the past to foreshadow, interpret, and illuminate a figure in the author's narrative. When Barack Obama was inaugurated as President of the United States, he swore the oath using Abraham Lincoln's Bible: the perhaps somewhat wishful typology was clear. So we shall see that for Matthew, Jesus is very much like Moses. For Luke, Mary is very much like her namesake Miriam, Moses's sister, who also sang about God's deliverance of God's people.

For Matthew, it is a gift that Joseph has the same name as the Joseph who is the main character in the last third of the book of Genesis. The Joseph of Genesis saw dreams and interpreted them; so does Joseph of Galilee. The Joseph of Genesis acted righteously and was a servant of God; so is Joseph of Galilee. The Joseph of Genesis goes to Egypt, and so does Joseph of Galilee, taking with him his wife and his adopted son. The earlier story helps us understand the later story; especially it helps us understand the way in which God acts and calls upon people to serve God righteously.

Only Matthew's Gospel tells the story of the magi from the East (Matt 2:1-12). In that story, too, we find indications of Jesus's particular significance in Matthew's Gospel.

Jesus Is the Surprising King

Every version of Jesus's story has to deal with the fact that the man claimed to be Messiah, and more, the man claimed to be the expected king like David and did not live in accord with any royal expectations. And as we shall see in the final chapters of this book, every version of Jesus's story has to deal especially with the fact that Jesus did not die in accord with any royal or messianic expectations.

The term Matthew uses for the visitors from the East—*magi*—does not really indicate that they were "kings," despite their representation in many paintings and despite the popularity of the Christmas carol "We Three Kings of Orient Are." They were more likely some kind of advisors. Their attention to the star may indicate a commitment to astrology. They also clearly represent economic power, judging from the value of the gifts they bring and the expense of the journey they undertake. And they are searching for political power: "Where is the newborn king of the Jews?" (Matt 2:2) they ask. Not surprising they seek kingship in the capital and not in Bethlehem.

The scene Matthew portrays opens up to all kinds of puzzles and paradoxes that are the familiar stuff of drama, opera, and poetry. The powerful come to worship the weak. The innocent baby threatens the guilty King Herod. The king of the Jews is born in humble circumstances far from the seat of power. Matthew's birth narrative is the story of a surprising king, a different Messiah, and the rest of his Gospel will reaffirm that theme.

Significantly, the magi are also not Jews. While Matthew's Gospel more than any other stresses Jesus's deep connection to the history of Israel and to the redemption of the Jewish people, from the beginning this story also indicates that Jesus is savior not only of his people but also of all people. When they worship the one who is born king of the Jews, they also become the first Gentiles to worship him. They are a sign that Jesus is Messiah and more.

The Gospel of Luke

Jesus Is the Focus of History

Matthew begins his Gospel with a genealogy. Luke begins the narrative in other ways that we shall soon note, but before long he, too, presents a back story to his main story. He, too, presents a genealogy in 3:23-38. Like Matthew, Luke traces Jesus's connection to David through Joseph. In the second chapter Luke had already explained Jesus's birth in Bethlehem as a result of Joseph's connection to the family of David (Luke 2:4). While Matthew validates Joseph as Jesus's father through Joseph's adoption of Mary's son, Luke simply acknowledges the tricky relationship between tracing Jesus's history through Joseph and insisting that Mary was a virgin when she conceived Jesus: "People supposed that [Jesus] was the son of Joseph" (Luke 3:23).

While Matthew begins his genealogy at the beginning of the family tree: "Abraham was the father of Isaac" (Matt 1:2), Luke begins with Jesus and works backward (3:23). However, for Luke, the first ancestor in the family line was not Abraham but Adam. Jesus's story is not simply the climax of the story of Israel, beginning with Abraham; it is the climax of the story of humankind, beginning with Adam. This is entirely in keeping with Luke's strong emphasis on the claim that Jesus is Lord of not only Israel but also all peoples. Matthew believes this too, but for him it is a subsidiary claim; for Luke, the inclusion of all people in God's saving care is a major theme. That is true not only in Luke's Gospel but also in the other book he probably wrote, the Acts of the Apostles.

When we move from the prequel to Jesus's story in Luke 3 to the beginning of the story itself in Luke 1 we notice that, like Mark, Luke needs to get to the story of Jesus by way of John the Baptist. However, unlike Mark, Luke gets to John the Baptist by way of John's parents.

The story of Zechariah and Elizabeth serves Luke's picture of Jesus in two ways. First, by telling us that John the Baptist was not only Jesus's forerunner but also his relative, Luke finds a biological as well as a theological way to insist on what all four New Testament Gospels insist—the meaning of Jesus for believers is closely tied to the story of John the Baptist.

Second, by telling the story of Zechariah and Elizabeth just before the story of Mary and the angel, Luke makes a claim that is central to his understanding of what God is doing for humankind in Jesus Christ. With God nothing will be impossible (see Luke 1:37). In these early chapters of Luke God does two impossible things. First, God gives a child to Elizabeth, who is beyond child-bearing years; second, God gives a child to Mary, who is a virgin. We saw that the story of the magi in Matthew 2:1-12 is a story of expectations overturned. The story of the two mothers in Luke 1 is a story of the world overturned, that is, God doing what no human could do.

We notice, too, in the first chapter of Luke's Gospel that Luke finds his own way to show how completely the story of Jesus fits the pattern and expectation of the Old Testament. The story is not full of scriptural quotations, like Matthew, nor of typology (though Mary does remind us of Miriam, Moses's sister, singing God's victory). What we get in Luke is a series of songs and psalms, which by their style and content remind us of the songs of the Old Testament. In musical dramas, today one way to hold the plot and the score together is to rely on the reprise, which is the song from the first act sung again in the second act to remind us where we are in the story and why.

Luke 1 is a kind of reprise of Old Testament songs—slightly altered for the altered action of the drama—but immediately familiar. This is

Luke's way of saying implicitly what Matthew says over and over again explicitly: the story of Jesus is the climactic act in the drama of God's dealing with Israel and through Israel with all of humankind. In order to understand Act Two, we need to refer back to Act One, time and time again.

Jesus Reverses Human History

We notice that as Joseph is the protagonist of Matthew's birth narrative, Mary is the protagonist of Luke's. In Matthew 1:25 it is Joseph the adoptive father who names his son Jesus. In Luke 1:31 it is Mary who is given the command to name the baby. In Matthew the stress on Jesus's miraculous conception is based on Matthew's belief in prophecy. Isaiah 7 has predicted that a virgin will conceive and bear a son, and now that scripture has been fulfilled.

For Luke the virgin birth is more a matter of genealogy than of prophecy. The reason the child can be called Son of God is that the Holy Spirit was the agent of his conception. So for Luke the claim that Jesus is Son of God has a kind of rooting in biology rather than in prophecy. In Luke 1:38, Mary is the first person to believe in the good news of Jesus Christ, when she accepts the promise of the angel. In Luke 1:46-55, Mary is the first person to proclaim the good news of Jesus Christ in the song she sings.[4] It is appropriate that this Gospel, which stresses the unity of Jews and Gentiles in the new community of faith, also foreshadows some equality of women and men: women and men believe; women and men preach.

Mary's song in Luke 1:46-55 provides rich evidence of what Jesus will mean for Luke:

> *With all my heart I glorify the Lord!*
> *In the depths of who I am I rejoice in God my Savior.*
> *He has looked with favor on the low status of his servant.*
> *Look! From now on, everyone will consider me highly favored*
> *because the mighty one has done great things for me.*
> *Holy is his name.*
> *He shows mercy to everyone,*

> *from one generation to the next,*
> *who honors him as God.*
>
> *He has shown strength with his arm.*
> *He has scattered those with arrogant thoughts and proud inclinations.*
> *He has pulled the powerful down from their thrones*
> *and lifted up the lowly.*
> *He has filled the hungry with good things*
> *and sent the rich away empty-handed.*
> *He has come to the aid of his servant Israel,*
> *remembering his mercy,*
> *just as he promised to our ancestors,*
> *to Abraham and to Abraham's descendants forever.*

The poem is the clearest declaration we have in Luke's Gospel of what the theologian Allen Verhey said was the major theme of hope in the New Testament: the Great Reversal.[5] Luke says that in Jesus all the expectations of worldly power and success are reversed; those who are cast out will be brought in; those who are downtrodden will be lifted up. Mary's poem like much Old Testament prophecy is written in the past tense as if all these things had already happened, but it is really a promise and prediction of what will come.

When we look in chapter 5 at some of the stories in Luke's Gospel we will see how much Luke insists on this claim that the coming of Jesus is not just a matter of personal faith or of getting together as a worshipping community. For Luke the coming of Jesus is the sign of a new world order. Jesus is the Christ because, as the Messiah was supposed to do, he brings a new world of justice and equity.

After the songs and prophecies of Luke 1, we turn to the most popular version of the birth of Jesus in Luke 2:1-20.

Again, we see themes that help us understand who Luke thinks Jesus is.

His birth, for instance, is the beginning of the great reversal. He is born outside the inn or the lodging because there is no room for him. Much has been written about the exact nature of housing options for travelers in the first century, but it is safe to say that when Jesus is born, he is born outside. Throughout Luke's Gospel Jesus will be both outsider and friend to the outsiders.

The shepherds who hear the message are themselves outsiders. Shepherds were not very high on the economic or social pecking order of their time, so in the world turned upside down it is almost as surprising that they get the good news as it was for a young virgin to hear that news.

The twofold song the angels sing is itself a good summary of who Jesus is in Luke's Gospel: "Glory to God in heaven" (2:14). Luke does not specify yet just how God is glorified in the coming of Jesus, but the rest of the story will be used to encourage and deepen the human desire to glorify God.

"Peace among those whom [God] favors" (2:14). Again as we have seen the promise of the baby is a promise of people coming together, not just before God, but with each other. Jesus makes a difference for the way we live our lives.

Finally, Jesus makes a difference for the larger world of politics, economics, and warfare. Luke has told us in the first verses of his Gospel that he sets out to be a historian, and like any good historian Luke wants to place the story of Jesus in the context of the "larger" world history. We know who the emperor was and who the governor was. We will know before the story is up that the world turned upside down will be turned upside down not just for individuals but for society, not just for the faithful but for the world.

The Gospel of John

For Mark, the beginning of his narrative is the preaching of John the Baptist and Jesus's own baptism, though Isaiah has prepared the way for the one who prepares the way. For Matthew, the story begins with Abraham, the Father of Israel. For Luke, the story begins with Adam, the first created person and the father of humankind.

For John, the story begins earlier yet. The first words are the first words of the book of Genesis, and the beginning is set even before the creation of the world: "In the beginning was the Word and the Word was with God and the Word was God. The Word was with God in the beginning. Everything came into being through the Word, and without the Word nothing came into being" (John 1:1-3).

John does not yet tell us that this is the story of Jesus, and for John the story of Jesus begins when "the Word became flesh and made his home among us" (John 1:14). It would be misleading to interpret John as saying: "In the beginning was Jesus and Jesus was with God and Jesus was God." The Word comes into human life in the birth of Jesus.

When John says that in the beginning was the Word, the term he uses is the Greek word *logos*. We use the same word in some of our English terms. *Bio-logy* is words about life, the study of life. *Theo-logy* is words about God, the study of God. When we use words correctly we are "logical."

When John talks about the Word being with God at the beginning, he is interpreting the Genesis story in which God creates everything by speaking, by using words, by using the Word: "Then God said, 'Let there be light.' And so light appeared. God said, 'Let there be lights in the dome of the sky to separate the day from the night'" (Gen 1:3, 14).

When John reads the creation story in Genesis he sees that God creates everything by the power of the word. "God said"—God used words—"and it was so." And when John talks about the Logos, about the Word, being with God from the beginning, he probably draws on two ideas that were common in his time.

First, he draws on the Jewish notion that from the beginning of time God has been accompanied by *wisdom*. The Greek word for *wisdom* (as John would have it in his Bible) was *sophia*, and in some of the later biblical books the writers claim that wisdom was present with God when God made the heavens and the earth. The word *sophia* is a word of the feminine gender in Greek. Though the genders of Greek words need not correspond in any direct way to the gender of the object being named, there is an early tradition that wisdom was female.

Sometimes it seems as though the claim that "wisdom" was present with God is poetical, a fancy way of saying that God planned wisely and had a clear plan in mind for the creation. And sometimes it seems as though wisdom is really seen as a kind of personified female who serves as divine companion to God—under God's authority but a kind of junior partner in the creation.⁶

Here Lady Wisdom speaks in Proverbs 8:22-23 and 29-31:

> *The LORD created me at the beginning of his way,*
> *before his deeds long in the past.*
>
> *I was formed in ancient times,*
> *and at the beginning, before the earth was.*
>
> . . . .
>
> *when he set a limit for the sea,*
> *so the water couldn't go beyond his command,*
> *when he marked out the earth's foundations.*
> *I was beside him as a master of crafts.*
> *I was having fun,*
> *smiling before him all the time,*
> *frolicking with his inhabited earth*
> *and delighting in the human race.*

And here is Proverbs 3:19: "The LORD laid the foundations of the earth with wisdom, establishing the heavens with understanding."⁷

Second, John apparently knows something of the teaching of the philosophers called the Stoics. For Stoics the *logos* was the plan, the blueprint by which the universe was put together. Not only was there a pattern, a *logos*, in the created world, but also there was a *logos* in the mind of each human being. The *logos* was the reasonable power by which people were able to understand the pattern and the blueprint of the world. Those who used their own *logos* to understand the *logos* of the world were those who were "logical." Somewhat similarly for Proverbs, not only does wisdom dwell with God, but also wisdom can be found in humans who use wisdom to discern the patterns and rules of creation.

Therefore drawing on Jewish writings and on Stoic philosophy John moves the story of Jesus back beyond John the Baptist and Isaiah and Abraham and Adam to the time before time. For John, the story of Jesus is first of all the story of creation. From the beginning God worked through God's Word toward the great climax of God's story—when in Jesus the world came to dwell among humankind.

In most Bibles today these first verses from John's Gospel are printed just the way they appear on pages 53–54. But many students of John's Gospel think that the first verses of John are a long poem, a hymn. Either they are a hymn that John knew and revised somewhat, or they are a hymn that John wrote and again probably revised to fit with the story he is telling.

When we are trying to understand Christology in the New Testament it helps to understand how Jesus began to be called Christ/Messiah and Son of God. It helps to see how the different Gospel writers begin their stories of Jesus. It also helps to see what early Christians said about Jesus in their poetry, what they sang about him in their hymns. These first verses of John are one such hymn, but there are other hymns in the letters of Paul and in Revelation. Strikingly some of the boldest claims about Jesus were not just preached; they were sung.

We will look at these hymns in our next chapter.

For Further Reading

Bartlett, David L. *What's Good about This News?* Louisville: Westminster John Knox, 2003.

Brown, Raymond. *The Gospel According to John.* Vol. 1. of The Anchor Bible Series. Garden City: Doubleday, 1966.

———. *The Birth of the Messiah.* New York: Doubleday, 1999.

Collins, Adela Y. *Mark (Hermeneia).* Minneapolis: Fortress, 2007.

Ringe, Sharon. *Wisdom's Friends: Community and Christology in the Fourth Gospel.* Louisville: Westminster John Knox, 1999.

Chapter 5
Singing about Jesus: Hymns and Prayers in the New Testament

We suggested in our first chapter that sometimes the best way to understand who Jesus is in the New Testament is not just to look at the titles the early Christian writers used for him but to look at his role in different kinds of Christian literature.

In this chapter we want to look at what first-century Christians sang about Jesus in their worship. Even in our time we can often learn about what people believe by the songs they sing more than we can by the official statements they make. Christian preaching may sound very much alike in a Presbyterian church and a Methodist church, but the favorite hymns will be different.

The early Christians showed what they believed about Jesus by what they sang about him. Perhaps equally important they showed what they believed about Jesus when they sang songs of praises to him, in much the same way that they sang praises to the creator God.

New Testament Hymns

Many students of the New Testament have noticed that books that were written in prose sometimes seem to be interrupted by passages that seem to be structured as poems.

The earliest manuscripts of the New Testament are all written in capital letters, with no punctuation and certainly no paragraphs or line divisions. If we were to redo the last sentence in the style of our New Testament manuscripts it would read:

THEEARLIESTMANUSCRIPTSOFTHENEWTESTAMENTA
REALLWRITTENINCAPITALLETTERSWITHNOPUNCTUA
TIONANDCERTAINLYNOPARAGRAPHSORLINEDIVISIONS.

The use of punctuation and paragraphs and the alignment of a passage on the page are the work of careful editors—both in our Greek editions of the New Testament and in the English and other modern translations.

In trying to capture the structure of the earliest Christian writings scholars have noticed that at a few places in the New Testament letters, in the Gospel of John, and in the book of Revelation the rhythm of the words seems to be repetitive and regular, more like a poem than like a typical letter.

Imagine a letter written or a post posted on Facebook by someone driving across the United States for the first time: "We have travelled now from Chicago through Kansas and Nebraska and arrived yesterday in Wyoming. Despite a flat tire and an unexpected detour we have enjoyed the trip. What a beautiful country! O beautiful, for spacious skies, for amber waves of grain. For purple mountains' majesty above the fruited plain!"

Years from now, if anyone is reading our Facebook posts, someone might notice that the paragraph takes on a fairly set rhythm halfway through. Though the reader might not be sure whether the rhythm shifts with "What a beautiful country!" or with "O beautiful, for spacious skies," she might notice that this is a different kind of writing.

For someone reading the Facebook post, the fact that two of the sentences rhyme is another clue that the writer is quoting some kind of poem or song. In the Greek of the first century of our era, poetry was not marked by rhyme, but it was marked by rhythm. It could be divided into stanzas and lines of fairly regular length and perhaps even fairly regular rhythm.

Some familiar American poems depend on rhythm, repetition, and structure but not on rhyme for their beauty. Here is the first stanza from Walt Whitman's great meditation on the death of Abraham Lincoln:

"When Lilacs Last in the Dooryard Bloom'd"

When lilacs last in the dooryard bloom'd,
And the great star early dropp'd in the western sky in the night,
I mourn'd and yet shall mourn with ever-returning spring.

Ever returning spring, trinity sure to me you bring,
Lilac blooming perennial and drooping star in the west,
And thought of him I love.[1]

Of course it is a matter of guesswork to try to reconstruct a poem that a New Testament writer is quoting, but for many scholars the guesswork has been informed by a knowledge of poetry in the first century. Furthermore, sometimes the language of the passage is somewhat different than the language that surrounds it. The vocabulary is different from the vocabulary in the rest of the letter or the Gospel or the book of Revelation. Words are repeated or one line seems to elaborate the line before. We cannot know for sure that these are poems or hymns, but it seems most likely that some passages include quotations from hymns; however, these quotations may have been changed for the purposes of the letter or of the Gospel.

Jack T. Sanders has suggested some of the stylistic clues that seem to indicate that a passage is a quotation from a hymn.[2] First, many of these passages begin with a relative pronoun—that is, *who*. Sanders suggests that this is because the hymns followed a time of praise in the worship of the church. So the leader might say something like: "We praise Jesus Christ." And then the congregation would sing the hymn:

> *"Who, though he was in the form of God,*
> *did not regard equality with God*
> *as something to be exploited." (Phil 2:6)*

Or the leader says: "We thank God for our Lord Jesus." And the congregation sings: "[*Who*] is the image of the invisible God, the firstborn of all creation" (Col 1:15).

The second feature is much more evident in the Greek text than in the English translations. Hymns tend to use participles instead of finite verbs. Here is a sentence with a participle: "I see a man *going* down the street." Here is almost the same sentence with a finite verb: "I see a man; he goes down the street."

Here are a few verses from the passage in Philippians, which may be a hymn, translating the participles in a wooden way:

(Jesus Christ)

Who, **existing** *in the form of God,*

Did not count equality with God a prize to be grasped,

But emptied himself,

Taking *the form of a slave*

And **being born** *in the likeness of humans. (Phil 2:6-7 AT)*

Here is a passage from Ephesians 2. It is harder to catch the participles in even a literal English translation because most are past participles. We'll try to indicate them by a bad translation and by bolding the participles:

(Jesus Christ is our peace)

The **maker** *of unity for us both*

And the **breaker down** *of the dividing wall of hostility" (Eph 2:14 AT)*

Third, these passages that seem to be hymns can be divided into verses. Of course, there is a great deal of guess work in these divisions, but we shall lay out each of our "hymn" passages in stanzas as best we can. You will see in some of them that they are different in style from the verses that come before them and after them, and that difference can best be signaled by dividing them into verses. Most of the earliest Christians would have listened to the Gospels or to the letters from Paul and others, and we can suspect that they would know when the rhythm of the language shifted—especially if it shifted into a poem or a hymn they already knew.

Try reading this paragraph aloud: "We visited our son in Japan during the early spring when, loveliest of trees, the cherry now was hung with blossoms on every bow, and after visiting a beautiful park we stopped for sushi." Even if we don't know that the lines about the cherry tree are from a poem by A. E. Housman we may recognize that the author has moved from a simple description of his visit to something more poetic.

When we discover a hymn or a poem embedded in a New Testament passage we are still left with several questions. First, did the author write this poem, or is he quoting someone else? Second, when the author quotes the poem, is he introducing it to his audience, or does he draw on a source that they already know? Does he perhaps choose a passage because it reaffirms claims that they already believe?

To this day when preachers want to gain the assent of their congregation they often quote a poem that is already familiar. Especially preachers will quote from a hymn that the congregation already knows. In this case familiarity often breeds consent. Especially in the powerful "celebration" passages that end many African-American sermons we can hear the echoes and often the direct quotation of hymns and choruses that are an essential part of the religious lives of the hearers and of the worship practices of the congregation.[3]

With the New Testament passages we are left with guesses. What follows in this chapter is a discussion of several passages in the New Testament that I follow many other scholars in guessing represent hymns or perhaps poems quoted by the New Testament writer.

I will make a guess or two about whether the author wrote the hymn or is quoting it, and in some cases I make a guess or two about how the author may have edited the hymn for the purposes of his own writing. In every case I want to suggest that often faith is formed more by how people pray and sing than by how people argue or preach or interpret scripture. By looking at these early Christian hymns we may get some sense of what believers were singing about Jesus even before they wrote letters or Gospels about him.[4]

Philippians 2:6-11

The earliest example we have of an early Christian hymn is Philippians 2:6-11. Paul writes to the Philippians mostly to praise their faith in Jesus and their friendship to Paul, but he is also concerned that there is some kind of tension within the community—some sense that the Philippians need to come to greater agreement and to think more highly of one another. As part of this appeal, Paul quotes a hymn. It seems likely that he did not compose the hymn for this occasion, because the vocabulary and style seem somewhat different from his usual vocabulary and style. Furthermore, it seems possible to notice those places where Paul edits the hymn to make his own points, to add his own emphasis.

Here is the admonition to the Philippians that leads up to that hymn: "Let not each of you consider only what concerns yourself, but also what concerns others. Have that mind among yourselves which you already have in Christ Jesus" (Phil 2:5 AT).

Then comes the hymn. Here is a guess on how the hymn might be divided into verses. The bolded words are probably an addition that Paul made to the original hymn:

> *[Christ Jesus]*
> *Who, though he existed in the form of God,*
> *Did not consider it a prize to be grasped*
> *To be equal to God.*
> *But emptied himself*
> *And took the form of a slave*
>
> *And was born in the likeness of humans.*
> *And when he was found in form as a man,*
> *He humbled himself,*
> *And became obedient to death—*
> ***(even death on a cross)***
> *Therefore indeed God has exalted him most highly*

> *And has bestowed on him the name*
> *That is above every name,*
> *So that at the name of Jesus,*
> *Every knee should bow*
> *Of those in heaven, and on earth, and beneath the earth,*
> *And every tongue should confess (that)*[5]
> *"Lord Jesus Christ"*
> *To the glory of God the Father.*[6] *(Phil 2:6-11 AT)*

Some interpreters think that this hymn was originally written to compare Jesus Christ to Adam. While Adam did "grab" the tree of the knowledge of good and evil in order to make himself equal to God, Jesus lived as a servant. As Adam was disobedient, Christ was obedient. While Adam was driven out of the garden, Jesus was exalted to the presence of God.[7]

Certainly Paul meditates on the relationship between Adam and Christ as Second Adam in Romans 5 and 1 Corinthians 15, though in neither the Philippians hymn nor Paul's application of the hymn is the relationship between Christ and Adam made explicit. If we look at the structure of the hymn itself we see rather a threefold movement first downward and then upward. The movement goes through the spheres "in heaven, on earth, and under the earth" (Phil 2:10) and ends when the inhabitants of each of those realms bow to Jesus.

The hymn begins in heaven where Jesus, though in God's likeness, does not claim equality to God. It goes to earth, when Christ empties himself in the incarnation by coming in the likeness of humans. It descends under the earth when Christ is obedient to death.

At the end of the hymn Christ is exalted and given the name above every name. What all the tongues proclaim in verse 11 might be: "That Jesus Christ is Lord" or "That the Lord is Jesus Christ."

The little English word *that* in most of our translations represents a Greek word that sometimes functions simply as a quotation mark (our Greek manuscripts did not use punctuation). In that case verse 11 would read: "And every tongue proclaim, [quote] 'Lord Jesus Christ!'" [end quote].

In any case the name that is above every name is not given before the journey to earth begins, nor is it the name *Jesus*, which is given when Christ humbles himself. It is given only at the conclusion of his journey from heaven to earth to the underworld to heaven again.

It seems most likely that the name above every name is the name *Lord*, and that this name is bestowed on Jesus only after his life, death, and ascension. We saw in chapter 2 that the early Christian use of the word *Lord* has at least two implications. First, to say that Jesus is Lord is to distinguish him from Caesar who in some first-century contexts was claimed to be Lord. Second, to say that Jesus is Lord is to give him the Greek name that the Greek Bible uses for God's mysterious name, written in Hebrew as *YHWH* but spoken as *adonai* ("my Lord") and translated into Greek by the same word we translate here as "Lord." In other words, God has given Jesus the unnameable name of God's own self.

Here, perhaps, at the end of our hymn Christ is given the honor he refuses to grasp at the beginning of the story. He is given God's own special name. Equality with God is not a prize to be grasped; it is an honor to be bestowed to the one who humbles himself even to death.

It seems, therefore, that Paul is quoting a hymn that is older than his letter to the Philippians. He may even be quoting a hymn that they all know. We have seen that such quotation can be a powerful means of persuasion. It is possible that he is "singing" a claim that he is not yet prepared to argue. First is the claim that Christ, Jesus, or the one who came to earth as Jesus existed before he was born into the world.

Second is the claim that Christ Jesus is now exalted to something very like equality with God the Father.

Third is the claim that Christ in the time before his incarnation on earth was close enough to God that he could resist the temptation to grasp equality with God. It would not make much sense to write that Johannes Brahms early on determined that he should not try to be a greater musician than Ludwig von Beethoven if the possibility was not at least something he could ponder. For most of us, the question never even comes up.

It is worth remembering that Paul is now quoting a hymn that was presumably sung less than twenty years after Jesus's crucifixion. It is also worth remembering that while Paul quotes this hymn about a savior who existed with God and has returned to God, he also knows perfectly well that Jesus was a visible, tangible, actual human being who lived among people not that long ago. Paul knows Jesus's brother James and Jesus's companions Peter and John; if he wanted to, Paul could ask them what was Jesus's favorite food and how tall Jesus was.

That odd mix between the undeniably human and the mysteriously godly Jesus is as old as the Christian faith.

John 1:1-14

I have suggested that it is fairly easy to reconstruct the content of the hymn Paul quotes and revises in Philippians 2 because both the content and the structure of the hymn follow a pattern—from heaven to earth to underneath the earth and then to heaven again.

While a great many students of John's Gospel believe that the first verses of the first chapter are based on some kind of hymn or poem, there is much less consensus about where the poem ends, about how it should be structured, and about what revisions the Gospel writer may have made in the poem or hymn he knew.[8] My own guess is that the material about John the Baptist is added by the writer of the Gospel, and the hymn-like rhythm seems to change with verse 15, so that I propose that verse 14 is the end of the original poem or hymn.

We also notice that two of Sanders's marks of an early hymn are missing from these first verses of John. The text does not begin with a relative pronoun: "Who was with God and who was God." It begins with a quotation from Genesis 1:1: "In the beginning." And the text is not particularly marked by participles.

What this text does do more clearly and powerfully than the other poems we are discussing is to provide a kind of meditation on scripture. In this case the prologue to John's Gospel is a meditation on the first chapter of the book of Genesis.

The prologue does differ from the language of the verses that follow it, and it does appear that we can divide much of the passage into stanzas, though there is very little agreement about exactly how to do so.

Here is my guess at what the hymn or poem looked like before the Gospel writer started quoting it and revising it.

In the beginning was the Word,
And the Word was with God,
And the Word was God.

He was in the beginning with God.
All things came into being through him,
And without him not one thing came into being.

What has come into being in him was life.
And the life was the light of all people.
The light shines in the darkness, and the darkness has not overcome it.

He was in the world,
And the world came into being through him.
He came to what was his own, and his own people did not accept him.

But to all who received him,
Who believed in his name,
He gave power to become the children of God.

Who were born, not of blood,
Nor of the will of the flesh, or of the will of a man,
But of God.

And the Word became flesh and dwelt among us
And we have seen his glory,
The glory as of a father's only son,
Full of grace and truth. (AT)

One reason we can guess that John used a poem or a hymn as a source for his prologue is that we can see places where it looks as though the Gospel writer has revised or expanded on his source. In the first chapter of John's Gospel, the author seeks to make clear that John the Baptist was not superior to Jesus or even equal to Jesus, but that his role was to testify to Jesus who was greater than he was.

In reading the prologue we can see several places where the author seems to add comments regarding John the Baptist that look as though they were asides or parenthetical additions. Furthermore, though our attempt to reconstruct the "original" poem is always a matter of guess work, according to our best guesses we can see that these same comments about John the Baptist interrupt the rhythm of the poem.

John 1:6-9 read like an editorial addition to an earlier song: "A man named John was sent from God. He came as a witness to testify concerning the light, so that through him everyone would believe in the light. He himself wasn't the light, but his mission was to testify concerning the light. The true light that shines on all people was coming into the world."

Then in verses 10-11 we return to a more poetic form: "The light was in the world, and the world came into being through the light, but the world didn't recognize the light. The light came to his own people, and his own people didn't welcome him."

Notice what the hymn tells us about early Christian belief in Jesus—whether the hymn was written by the Gospel writer and then revised or inherited by him and then revised. First, the hymn is a meditation on the first chapter of the book of Genesis. The first words are "in the beginning" and are an exact quotation from the first two words of the book of Genesis in the first-century Greek edition. Genesis 1:1 then goes on to say: "God began to create the heavens and the earth." John 1:1 goes on to say: "was the Word, and the Word was with [next to, up against] God, and the Word was God."

Second, the poem plays especially on the claim in Genesis 1 that God created everything by speaking. In Hebrew the letters of the verb "to speak" are the same as the letters of the noun *word*. John knows that in the beginning was "the word" because in the beginning God "spoke" or God "worded." Genesis tells us so. We have seen how this claim that the Word was with God is interpreted in the context of Jewish and Greek writings in the first century of our era.

Third, while there is some disagreement about whether the hymn in Philippians 2 suggests that Christ existed with God before Jesus came to earth, in John 1 there is absolutely no question that this is the case. The Christian doctrine of "incarnation"—the claim that One who existed with God came to earth as a human being—is grounded above all in John 1:14: "The Word became flesh and made his home among us." (The Greek word is somewhat richer, "tented among us," "tabernacled among us," as the glory of God tented among the wandering Hebrews in the book of Exodus.)

Fourth, this Word that will be incarnate, en-fleshed, in Jesus was "with God and was God." The Greek is sufficiently nuanced—or ambiguous—here that Christian thinkers from the first century to the twenty-first have disagreed about how best to interpret it. What seems fair to say is that for the writer of this poem and for John who quotes it, the Word is so close to God that people can't talk about the Word without talking about God as well.

We are not sure whether these verses may originally have been a hymn or whether they were some other sort of poetry. What we have seen and will see is that hymns about Jesus in Philippians and Colossians were probably originally hymns *to* Jesus. Both those hymns and this poem suggest that for these early Christians it was appropriate not only to pray *through* Jesus, the Son or the Word, but also to pray *to* Jesus, the Son of the Word. In traditional Christian services today, believers often pray, "Praise to you, Lord Christ." And when Christians confess their sins, they pray, "Lord have mercy upon us; Christ have mercy upon us." The question of how Jesus is related to the creator God has from the first century on been in large measure this question: Can Christians pray to Jesus? If the Word is with God, if the Word *is* God, then the answer to that question is yes.

Fifth, it is through the Word—not just through speaking but through the Word who will be incarnate in Jesus—that God created all things, the universe. For John, the Christ is not created; he is cocreator with the one he calls Father. So talk about Jesus is not only talk about the one who taught in Galilee or even talk about the one who is crucified and risen again, but also talk about the incarnation of the Word, the Son, who joined the Father in creating the world and all that is in it.

Sixth, at least implicitly, this means that the world is created according to the pattern of Christ himself. To understand him rightly is to understand the shape and drama of creation. To see the shape and drama of creation rightly is to see Christ. This is because to say that Christ was the *logos* is not only to say that he was and is God's wisdom and was and is God's logic but also to say that he was and is the pattern, the blueprint, and the scheme by which creation was made.

To this day Christians who take John 1 as a fundamental statement about Jesus claim that the Word that was incarnate in Jesus existed before the creation of the world. That Word shared in creating the world, and the world was shaped to look like the Word itself. Of course, for John it was a smaller world that God created, but those who see themselves as John-like Christians now hold that the whole cosmos, in its unfathomable infinity, still carries the shape of the Word who became flesh, of Christ Jesus.

Colossians 1:15-20

To many students of the New Testament it seems likely that Colossians was written, not by Paul, but by one of his followers writing in his name. In any case the poem or hymn that we find in Colossians 1 seems to represent an understanding of Christ rather different than what we find in Philippians and I would suggest rather later in the development of Christian faith.

In Philippians 2 and John 1 there was good reason to believe that the author of the book was quoting from a hymn or a poem but also editing it for his own purposes. In Philippians 2, Paul stresses the importance of the cross, in a kind of add-on to the hymn. In John 1, John interrupts the poem for several verses about John the Baptist. Here is a reconstruction of the hymn from Colossians:

> *(Who) is the image of the invisible God,*
> *the firstborn of all creation.*
> *For in him all things in heaven and on earth were created [or "by him"]*
> *Things visible and invisible, whether thrones or dominions or rulers or powers—*
> *All things have been created through him and for him.*
>
> *He himself is before all things,*
> *And in him all things hold together.*
> *(He is the head of the body, the church.)*
> *He is the beginning, the firstborn from the dead,*
> *So that he might come to have first place in everything.*
>
> *For in him the fullness of God was pleased to dwell*
> *And through him God was pleased to reconcile to himself all things*
> *Whether on earth or in heaven,*
> *By making peace through the blood of his cross. (AT)*

The author of Colossians is particularly concerned with the relationship between Christ and the church. While we have seen that guesses about rhythm and verse are always tricky, it does seem that the author may have added at least one line to an existing hymn: "He is the head of the body, the church" (v. 18).

Further, some scholars have held that thematically and rhythmically the second line of verse 20 is the letter writer's addition to the original hymn: "by making peace through the blood of his cross."

The rest of the passage has some of the marks that Jack T. Sanders argues characterize an early Christian hymn or poem. Like Philippians 2:6 the passage begins with the relative pronoun *who*, so here the New Revised Standard Version translation is a little misleading: "He is the image of the invisible God." More literally Colossians 1:15 does not read, "He is the image of the invisible God," but, "Who is the image of the invisible

God."[9] In the context of Colossians 1, the use of the relative pronoun *who* makes perfectly good sense. The author has been referring to the "Son" who has rescued us from the power of darkness, and verse 15 continues the description of Christ, the Son "who is the image of…"

If Sanders is right that we have here an early Christian hymn, whether written by the same author as the letter, or by someone else, we may be able to guess that it had a context in worship. The worship leader would begin the hymn by saying or singing something like: "Praise to the Lord Jesus Christ." And then the congregation would respond by beginning the hymn: "Who is the image of the invisible God."

Furthermore, halfway through this passage we have another use of the relative pronoun *who*: "Who is the beginning, the first born from the dead" (v. 18b). In our tentative reconstruction of the hymn we will represent this line as the first line of the second stanza.

Perhaps most significant, these verses seem to provide a kind of series of stanzas of roughly the same length. They can be turned more easily into poetic form than the rest of Colossians, and indeed in the Greek editions of the New Testament, the authors often present the text in just that way. We translate from the twenty-seventh edition of the Nestle-Aland (Novum Testamentum Graece) text of the New Testament, dividing the lines as the editors of the Greek text have done:

> *Who is the image of the invisible God,*
> *The firstborn of all creation,*
> *Because in him all things were created, [or "by him"]*
> *In the heavens and on the earth.*
>
> *All things visible and invisible,*
> *Whether thrones or dominions*
> *Whether powers or authorities,*
> *All things were created through him and for him.*
>
> *He himself is before all things,*
> *And in him all things hold together.*

II.
Who is the beginning,
The firstborn from the dead,
In order that he might have first place among everything.
Because in him all the fullness of what is [or, of God?] was pleased to dwell,
And through him to reconcile all things to himself,
Whether on earth or in heaven.

Notice again the themes of this hymn. As in John's Gospel, the Word is in the beginning with God. In Colossians, it is God's beloved son, who is not precisely prior to creation, but the very first fruits of creation—as he will be the first fruits of resurrection. In Pauline language, Christ is both the first fruits of creation and the first fruits of the new creation. As he was the first to be brought forth from nothingness (at the beginning of time), he is the first to be brought forth from death (at the end).

Furthermore, as in John's Gospel, there is the clear claim that the Son was joined with the Father in creating the world. While it is not explicitly stated that creation is made in the image of Christ, the Son is the image, the icon of the Father.

In Genesis, Adam and Eve are made in the image of God. For Colossians, Christ has already borne that image. So implicitly Adam and Eve are made not only in the image of God but also in the image of Christ; and since all things come together in Christ, all creation bears that image too. We do not have any specific reference to the incarnation, to the Son coming in the flesh, as we do in the hymn of Philippians 2 and at least in the larger context of John 1. But since the Son is the visible image of the invisible God, it is clear not only that the Son exists at the beginning of creation and at the end but also that the Son has made the Father visible in the midst of creation.

Furthermore, the reference to the crucifixion in verse 20—"by making peace through the blood of his cross"—whether or not it is part of the original hymn, clearly grounds the letter's understanding of Christ in his earthly life, and the claim that he is first born from the dead is Colossians's way of proclaiming what Paul proclaims about the man Jesus, that on the third day he rose from the dead. For early Christians, this is not just a claim about divine glory but a claim about a great reversal in the course of human life. For this hymn the Son is the one who brings together and reconciles what seems to be separate. In him all people can come together. But more than that, in him the whole world hangs together. There is a pattern to all things, and the shape of that pattern is Jesus Christ.

Again we are suggesting that in the hymns and poems of the early church Christians not only sang about Jesus but also gave themselves the right to sing praise to him, and they declared him worthy of all praise because he was the image of the invisible God or the Word from the beginning or the one who, though in the form of God, did not count equality with God something to be grasped.

Before moving to the hymns in the book of Revelation we note one passage in Paul's letters that shows no clear evidence of being from a hymn or poem but fits some of our themes. This verse sounds like the kind of formula that early Christians might use in worship: "Yet for us there is one God, the Father, from whom are all things and for whom we exist, and one Lord, Jesus Christ, through whom are all things and through whom we exist" (1 Cor 8:6). This sounds like Paul simply assuming what John 1 and Colossians 1 both claim: that Christ was with God before the worlds came to be and that he was coauthor of the creation. In traditional terms this is a very "high" Christology in that it makes Jesus very nearly equal to God, the Son very much like the Father. It is striking again that this is a claim being made as early as the fifties of the Common Era, perhaps twenty or twenty-five years after Jesus's ministry and death.

Revelation 5:12-13

The book of Revelation is the last book in our editions of the New Testament, and it was probably one of the last of these books to be written. The book is written by a man named John, almost certainly not the John who is traditionally claimed as the author of the Fourth Gospel and almost certainly not John the Elder who wrote the letters of John. The author is on the isle of Patmos, and he writes to warn, encourage, or discipline Christians. My best guess is that the book was written toward the end of the first century CE.

The book begins when the resurrected Christ appears to John. The description of the risen Jesus in Revelation 1:12-16 is strikingly different from our usual expectations about what the risen Jesus might look like. Here he is described with images from the Old Testament that strongly link him to certain depictions of God in all God's holiness: "His head and hair were as white as white wool—like snow—and his eyes were like a fiery flame. His feet were like fine brass that has been purified in a furnace, and his voice sounded like rushing water" (Rev 1:14-15).

This Son of Man, the risen Jesus, tells John to write letters to seven churches in Asia Minor, praising or condemning the churches, often around issues of idolatry and their involvement with the larger society around them. Then beginning with Revelation 4:1, John presents a vision that he has received—a vision about the coming of God's rule on earth. Contained within the long vision, which extends from chapter 4 to the end of the book in chapter 21, are many quotations or references to earlier works. References to Ezekiel and to Isaiah are especially prominent.

However, there is another kind of quotation or allusion here. It seems likely that the many songs and words of praise contained in this book represent actual hymns sung in the worshipping communities of Asia Minor. The heavenly host sings hymns that the earthly church would recognize as their own. Heaven and earth mirror each other. (See, for instance, Rev 11:15-18 and Rev 15:3-4.)

They cried out with a loud voice:

> "Victory belongs to our God
> who sits on the throne,
> and to the Lamb.
>
> . . . .
>
> "Amen! Blessing and glory
> and wisdom and thanksgiving

> *and honor and power and might*
> *be to our God forever and always. Amen." (Rev 7:10, 12)*

Most of Revelation's hymns are directed to God the Father in praise, but one at least is directed to Christ. Because this is quoted as a hymn we do not need to ask, as we did with Philippians, John, and Colossians, where the editor has edited or adapted the hymn to his context. The hymn has two stanzas, and as John of Patmos says, as it is sung in heaven we may guess that he had heard it sung on earth:

> *Worthy is the slaughtered Lamb*
> *to receive power, wealth, wisdom, and might*
> *and honor, glory, and blessing. (Rev 5:12)*

(It may help us to understand this as a hymn if we listen to Handel's *Messiah* in which, in a slightly different translation, these words are set to music.)

The second stanza is sung by the same congregation, or perhaps it is sung antiphonally: some sing stanza A, while others respond with stanza B. This would mirror the heavenly worship during which angels sing stanza A and the creation responds with stanza B:

> *Blessing, honor, glory, and power belong*
> *to the one seated on the throne*
> *and to the Lamb,*
> *forever and always. (v. 13)*

With this hymn we do not need to reconstruct the opening invocation to praise as we did the hymns from Philippians and Colossians, because this is itself a song of praise.

We have seen that Philippians (and Colossians and to some extent John) tells a story that begins with Christ at the creation, descended to earth, slain, and then glorified, ascending to be with God again. Revelation's hymn does not include the first movement in that drama. There is no explicit reference to the Lamb existing before the beginning of time. The other movements of the drama, however, are recapitulated here:

- The one who lived on earth and was crucified, the Lamb, has now been exalted.
- All the praise that could be given to the Father is now given to the Son.
- The Son is designated as like God the Father because the angels and the creation can and should sing praise to both of them.
- Worship comes before doctrine, and in worship the Lamb is the exalted one; he is worthy of the same blessing as the Ancient of Days, God the Father, seated on the throne.

Again it is in the hymns and poems of the early church that we find most clearly a "high" Christology. Jesus's crucifixion is the warrant for his exaltation to stand by the throne of God. Because he has died and been elevated he is worthy of all praise; Christians not only sing *about* Jesus Christ but also sing *to* him. Power and wealth and wisdom and might and honor and glory and blessing are rightly his.

Faith is as much a matter of what believers sing as it is a matter of the stories they tell or the creeds they recite. In these hymns we see that very early in the life of the Christian communities believers sang *about* Jesus and sang *to* Jesus as one who shares in the very life of God.

For Further Reading

Brown, Raymond. *The Gospel According to John.* Vol. 1 of The Anchor Bible Series. Garden City: Doubleday, 1966.

Collins, Adela Yarbro. *Crisis and Catharsis: The Power of the Apocalypse.* Philadelphia: Westminster, 1984.

Cousar, Charles B. *Philippians and Philemon.* Louisville: Westminster John Knox, 2009.

Dunn, J. D. G. *Christology in the Making.* 2nd ed. Grand Rapids: Eerdmans, 1981.

Sanders, Jack T. *The New Testament Christological Hymns: Their Historical Religious Background.* Cambridge: Cambridge University Press, 1971.

Sumney, Jerry L. *Colossians: A Commentary.* Louisville: Westminster John Knox, 2008.

Chapter 6

Practical Christology: Paul and His Letters

The Apostle Paul was a follower of Jesus who joined the circle of believers only after Jesus's death and resurrection. We can tell from some of his writings that for some early Christians his authority was not as great as that of the circle of apostles who knew Jesus during his ministry—people like Peter and James and John.

What is striking about his decision to follow Jesus is that in the first years of the Christian movement, Paul had been a strong opponent of the church.

Paul's letters, however, are the earliest Christian writings we have. They date from about 50 CE. And Paul has long been seen as the most subtle and influential theologian of the New Testament writers. His writings shaped the theologies of such memorable theologians as Augustine of Hippo, Martin Luther, John Calvin, and Karl Barth.

Much has been written about Paul's Christology—his doctrine of who Jesus was and is for believers. However, in this book in which we are asking how and why claims about Jesus got made by the early Christians what may be most striking is this: Paul did not really develop a systematic Christology. We cannot draw up an outline of a perfectly consistent sent of claims Paul wanted to make about Jesus.

Paul was a theologian, but he was what we would call today a "practical theologian." That is, he did not write his theology as a set of propositions about God and Jesus. Nor did he write primarily as an interpreter of Scripture (for him the Hebrew Bible). He wrote primarily as a church founder and in response to problems in the earliest Christian churches and sometimes even to answer explicit questions that those churches had sent him.

Paul makes astonishing claims about Jesus, but he does not make these claims as part of an essay on Christology; he sets them out—sometimes almost tosses them out as asides—in the midst of the discussion of quite concrete and practical problems. For him Christology doesn't simply inform the beliefs of faithful people; it shapes their lives and influences their decisions.

In this chapter we shall look at five practical situations that Paul addresses and ask not just what his Christology was in these circumstances, but how that Christology works.

Why Contribute Generously to the Offering? 2 Corinthians 8:1-14

One of Paul's great concerns as he travelled around the Greek-speaking world founding and strengthening churches was to provide financial support for the struggling churches in Jerusalem. In writing to the church at Corinth Paul urges them to meet their pledge, fulfill their obligation, and give generously. He is sending his companion, Titus, to gather the offering.

Paul uses some of the traditional techniques of any fund-raiser. He uses a little guilt: are you living up to your own promises? He uses a little competitive spirit: have you noticed how generous those churches in Macedonia have been? Surely you can do as well. But he also uses a moving description of the significance of Jesus Christ for the lives of those who follow him:

> Brothers and sisters, we want to let you know about the grace of God that was given to the churches of Macedonia. While they were being tested by many problems, their extra amount of happiness and their extreme poverty resulted in a surplus of rich generosity. I assure you that they gave what they could afford and even more than they could afford, and they did it voluntarily. They urgently begged us for the privilege of

sharing in this service for the saints. They even exceeded our expectations, because they gave themselves to the Lord first and us, consistent with God's will. As a result, we challenged Titus to finish this work of grace with you the way he had started it. Be the best in this work of grace in the same way that you are the best in everything, such faith, speech, knowledge, total commitment, and the love we inspired in you.

I'm not giving an order, but by mentioning the commitment of others, I'm trying to prove the authenticity of your love also. You know the grace of our Lord Jesus Christ. Although he was rich, he became poor for our sakes, so that you could become rich through his poverty. I'm giving you my opinion about this. It's to your advantage to do this, since you not only started to do it last year but you wanted to do it too. Now finish the job as well so that you finish it with as much enthusiasm as you started, given what you can afford. A gift is appreciated because of what a person can afford, not because of what that person can't afford, if it's apparent that it's done willingly. It isn't that we want others to have financial ease and your financial difficulties, but it's a matter of equality. At the present moment, your surplus can fill their deficit so that in the future their surplus can fill your deficit. In this way there is equality.

Verse 9 can be translated in two ways, each of which is appropriate to Paul's plea for generosity; we can guess that Paul knew full well that his phrase had two complementary meanings. Here is the first translation: "For you know the generous act of our Lord Jesus Christ, that though he was rich, yet for your sakes he became poor, so that by his poverty you might become rich" (NRSV).

Paul is surely here referring to a more cosmic story than the earthly life of Jesus. In fact there is no evidence either in the Gospels or in any of Paul's writings that Jesus of Nazareth was particularly rich. Jesus does allude to his poverty in the saying, "Foxes have dens, and the birds in the sky have nests, but the Human One has no place to lay his head" (Matt 8:20; Luke 9:58). But there is no evidence that this saying contrasts Jesus's state with some earlier comfort, and there is no evidence that Paul knew this saying or anything like it. Rather, Jesus's wealth must have been the wealth of his status with God, and his act of generosity was to come as a human being into the midst of human history. The result of his generosity is that believers may have a richer (though not necessarily a wealthier) life on earth and that, presumably, they may also one day attain the riches of eternal presence with God.

The other way to translate the verse is this: "For you know the grace of our Lord Jesus Christ, that though he was rich, yet for your sake he became poor, so that by his poverty you might [be made] rich" (RSV).

Grace is the term that Paul uses to describe the whole activity of God in Jesus Christ. Grace is undeserved kindness and unexpected love. Grace is the unconditional favor with which God brings new life and hope to humankind in Jesus Christ. The folk hymn that has become a part of both church and popular culture catches something of the power of the term for Paul: "Amazing grace, how sweet the sound / that saved a wretch like me; / I once was lost but now I'm found / was blind but now I see." *Grace* becomes the all-encompassing word for the story of God's mercy to people in Jesus Christ.

Earlier in this same letter Paul emphasizes the power and majesty of grace: "We do this because we know that the one who raised the Lord Jesus will also raise us with Jesus, and he will bring us into his presence along with you. All these things are for your benefit. As grace increases to benefit more and more people, it will cause gratitude to increase, which results in God's glory" (2 Cor 4:14-15).[1] Now it is not only a specific act of kindness but also the whole story of God's activity in Jesus Christ for the sake of believers and then for the world that should inspire the Corinthians to generosity.

Paul's practical Christology works here in at least two ways. First, Christians are to imitate Christ; their acts of generosity are a response to his generous act and a re-presentation of that generosity for the sake of others. Second, Christians participate in the grace-filled life of Christ. They do what they do because they are who he is. They live out the grace that they have received. They do not simply follow Jesus's example; they live out his story.

In response to a practical need—to increase the offering for the Jerusalem Christians—Paul invokes an image that in turn recapitulates the whole story of Jesus, present with God, but giving himself for the sake of the world, to bring the whole world finally into the presence of God as well.

What Do We Do about Vegetarians? Romans 14

The Epistle to the Romans is the only letter we have of Paul's that was written to a church he did not found. This letter is written to the Roman churches to prepare the way for his coming visit to them, and he spends a good deal of the letter introducing them both to himself and to the content of his preaching and teaching. As we saw in looking at 2 Corinthians and will see again when we look at 1 Corinthians, in some of his letters it is quite clear precisely what issues Paul is addressing and equally clear that he knows a good deal about what is going on in the churches that will receive his letters.

Much of the letter to the Romans seems to be a more general statement of Paul's theological principles, but there is at least one issue in the congregation that he seems to acknowledge and then to address. There appears to be tension in the Roman congregations between believers who are ethnically Jews and those who are ethnically Gentiles. The Gentiles are apparently in the majority, and there appears to be some question about whether they are sufficiently welcoming when it comes to the Jewish Christians in their midst. The summary prescription for this problem is found in Romans 15:7: "So welcome each other, in the same way that Christ also welcomed you, for God's glory." As in 2 Corinthians 8 we have a strong claim made about the important work of Jesus Christ, but it is simply asserted and not developed into anything like a full-fledged Christology.

The assertion, however, has rich possibilities for understanding Paul. The church through the years has developed quite full doctrines of Jesus as the sacrifice to God, as the incarnation of God, and as the ransom for sin. Here Paul simply alludes to another way of understanding the function of Jesus Christ. Jesus is the one in whom believers are welcomed into the household of God; Jesus Christ is God's hospitality come in human form.

It seems likely that some of the more concrete issues Paul discusses earlier in Romans—especially in chapters 13 and 14—also reflect some actual information about what is going on among the Roman Christians. And it also seems likely that some of these concrete issues grow out of the tension between Gentile and Jewish Christians in Rome.[2] For instance, one issue seems to be what kind of food believers should serve when they are at common meals. Jewish Christians presumably believed in keeping the laws for a kosher diet; Gentile Christians did not.

Another issue is whether or not to observe certain days as sacred. While it is not clear that the issue is whether or not to keep the Jewish Sabbath, in our context that seems the most likely explanation of the controversy.

Paul writes to address both these disputes:

> Welcome the person who is weak in faith—but not in order to argue about differences of opinion. One person believes in eating everything, while the weak person eats only vegetables. Those who eat must not look down on the ones who don't, and the ones who don't eat must not judge the ones who do, because God has accepted them [or "welcomed them"]. Who are you to judge someone else's servants? They stand or fall before their own Lord (and they will stand, because the Lord has the power to make them stand).
>
> One person considers some days to be more sacred than others, while another person considers all days to be the same. Each person must have their own convictions. Someone who thinks that a day is sacred, thinks that way for the Lord. Those who eat, eat for the Lord, because they thank God. And those who don't eat, don't eat for the Lord, and they thank the Lord too.
>
> We don't live for ourselves and we don't die for ourselves. If we live, we live for the Lord [or "to the Lord"], and if we die, we die for the Lord [or "to the Lord"]. Therefore, whether we live or die, we belong to [the Lord]. This is why Christ died and lived: so that he might be Lord of both the dead and the living. (Rom 14:1-9)

Some years ago, a rabbi friend suggested that in his community one way to solve the issue of what to serve, when some observed kosher rules and some did not, was to serve communal meals that were vegetarian. Such meals provided something for everyone. Whether that is the precise question for the Roman Christians, it does seem that Paul has heard that there are some vegetarians in the community and some vegetarian despisers. It might seem to us that the vegetarians are "stronger" in faith since they are more demanding of themselves than the omnivores, but for Paul, being "strong in faith" has a different connotation.

Those who are weak in faith for Paul are those who believe that in order to be assured of God's favor they need to engage in some practices that prove their faithfulness. People who are weak in faith eat vegetables to stay kosher. They keep Sabbath religiously. As we see elsewhere in Paul's writings, the weak in faith won't eat meat that has been used in pagan temple sacrifices, lest that displease God. The strong in faith believe that God's favor does not depend on such practices, and so they gladly roast leftover sacrificial animals and enjoy the feast that follows (see 1 Cor 8:1-13).

Here, however, Paul does not use his claims about Jesus as Christ in order to strengthen the claims of the strong in faith. As we have noted he is more concerned with welcoming—with diminishing the distinctions that are separating one Christian community from another. The reason that Paul can insist on the unity of the church is that unity is found, not in friendliness, or in common practices, or even in simple good manners. The unity of the church is found in its Lord, Jesus: "We don't live to ourselves and we do not die to ourselves. If we live we live to the Lord and if we die, we die to the Lord. Therefore, whether we live or whether we die we belong to the Lord. This is why Christ died and lived: so that he might be Lord of both the dead and the living" (Rom 14:7-9).[3]

Notice how many claims about Christ and his significance are contained in these brief sentences.

First, the grounding of Christian life both in this world and in the world to come is the story of Jesus's death and resurrection. He identifies with believers in his living, in his dying, and in his living again. He is the Lord of believers, the holy one, and the true ruler, in their living, their dying, and in their living again. For this reason, nothing can separate believers from the love of God. Those who believe in Christ belong to Christ, and death does not change that.

Furthermore, because believers are one in Jesus Christ, they are one in each other. Their differences—keeping Sabbath or not, eating meat or not—are entirely insignificant compared to their unity, their shared existence in Jesus Christ.

Finally, there is a strong statement about the nature and power of death, not nearly so elaborate as we shall see in 1 Corinthians 15 but stark in its own certainty. The reason that death is not the end for believers is that Christ is Lord both of life and of death, of what is and of whatever is to come.

In the verses leading up to this affirmation there is one more christological claim. Jesus stands as Lord who will be judge of the living and the dead. Not only will all believers live in him, but also all will stand before him for a final accounting—whether on the day of our death or on the last day of history. "Who are you to judge someone else's servants? They stand or fall before their own Lord (and they will stand, because the Lord has the power to make them stand)" (Rom 14:4).

What Happens When We Die? 1 Corinthians 15

For the most part, in reading Paul's letters to various churches, we get only his side of the conversation. When he writes 1 Corinthians, however, Paul gives us important information about what the Corinthians are asking him.

He has two sources of information about the church at Corinth. The Corinthian believers have sent him a letter filled with questions, and often he quotes these questions before answering them. And a delegation from the church, designated as "Chloe's people," has come in person bringing further information about the congregation and raising further questions.

The last of the issues that Paul addresses directly in this letter is raised in 1 Corinthians 15:12: "Now if Christ is proclaimed as raised from the dead, how can some of you say that there is no resurrection of the dead?" The claim some Corinthians are making seems straightforward enough: "[There is] no resurrection of the dead." However, in fact, there are at least three ways of understanding their claim, and some scholars have defended each one of these.

The interpretation that seems most obvious to us, perhaps because it is most prevalent in our own time, is simply this: when we die, we die, and that is the end of it. No heaven, no afterlife, no resurrection to a new existence. We are remembered for as long as there are people to remember us, and then nothing. This sounds like the kind of belief of the Corinthians Paul quotes in 15:32: "let's eat and drink because tomorrow we'll die."

A second interpretation reminds us that in the first century, as now, there were many people who believed that the human being was divided into a body and a soul. When we die, they claimed, the body decays but the soul remains. Then, as now, there are many different theories about what happens to the soul, but then as now the belief in immortality depended on a distinction between the material body and the spiritual soul. But those who believe in the immortality of the soul don't really believe in the resurrection from the dead, which involves the whole person, not just the soul.

A third interpretation relies very much on a reading of the first chapters of 1 Corinthians. At some points in that letter it looks as though the mistake Paul believes the Corinthians are making is that they think they have something very like eternal life right now: "Already you have all you want! Already you have become rich! Apart from us you rule; indeed I wish that you did rule, so that we might rule with you" (1 Cor 4:8 AT). These interpreters claim that the Corinthians believe what the Gospel of John sometimes seems to claim: that eternal life is right now, and the faithful do not need to wait for some kind of future consummation.

Whatever the exact mistake Paul thinks the Corinthians are making, his response involves a particular interpretation of Jesus's life, death, and resurrection, and of what the life, death, and resurrection mean for believers when they die:

> So if the message that is preached says that Christ has been raised from the dead, then how can some of you say, "There's no resurrection of the dead"? If there's no resurrection of the dead, then Christ hasn't been raised either. If Christ hasn't been raised, then our preaching is useless and your faith is useless. We are found to be false witnesses about God, because we testified against God that he raised Christ, when he didn't raise him if it's the case that the dead aren't raised. If the dead aren't raised, then Christ hasn't been raised either. If Christ hasn't been raised, then your faith is worthless; you are still in your sins, and what's more, those who have died in Christ are gone forever. If we have a hope in Christ only in this life, then we deserve to be pitied more than anyone else.

But in fact Christ has been raised from the dead. He's the first crop of the harvest of those who have died. Since death came through a human being, the resurrection of the dead came through one too. In the same way that everyone dies in Adam, so all will be made alive in Christ. Each event will happen in the right order: Christ, the first crop of the harvest, then those who belong to Christ at his coming, and then the end, when Christ hands over the kingdom to God the Father, when he brings every form of rule, every authority and power to an end. It is necessary for him to rule until he puts all enemies under his feet. Death is the last enemy to be brought to an end, since he has brought everything under control under his feet. When it says that everything has been brought under his control, this clearly means everything except for the one who placed everything under his control. But when all things have been brought under his control, then the Son himself will also be under the control of the one who gave him control over everything so that God may be all in all. (1 Cor 15:12-28)

This is obviously a much more complicated argument than the brief affirmations we saw in 2 Corinthians 8 and Romans 14. Again, here are a few of the claims that Paul is making about Jesus's significance in the face of death. First, in 1 Corinthians 15:1-8, Paul appeals to what the Corinthians already believe. He assumes that they believe that Christ is risen from the dead, not as a soul but as a person. They believe this because it is what was preached to them and because they know of those—Peter and James and a host of others—who had seen the risen Lord.

Second, and here is where Paul begins to make his own christological claims, Jesus cannot have been the only case of resurrection from the dead. Paul believes that God has promised resurrection to all the faithful at the end of time, and Jesus's resurrection cannot be an odd and unique event; it is the first event in the great cosmic last act that Paul has believed in all along. So for Paul, Jesus's resurrection does not just tell us something about Jesus; Jesus's resurrection introduces the whole drama at the end of time.

Third, Paul believes that in order to understand the story of Jesus we need to understand the story of Adam. We have seen that for the Gospel of Matthew, Joseph, the son of Jacob, is a kind of "type" of Joseph, Mary's husband. It is also the case that for Matthew, Moses becomes a "type" of Jesus. He foreshadows who Jesus will become (see chapter 8).

For Paul, Adam is a "type" of Jesus. To read Adam right is to see him as foreshadowing Jesus; to read Jesus right is to see him as recapitulating and reversing the story of Adam. Further, for Paul, the story of Adam is not just a story of one person; it is the story of humankind. And from Genesis 2–3 on it has been clear that like Adam (or even "in Adam") every human being is bound to die.

The way God reverses what Adam has done, as representative of humankind, is to send Jesus as a representative of humankind. Adam, by disobeying God's command, brought death to everyone. Christ, by obeying, brings life to everyone. This is not a systematic Christology, but it is a powerful picture, a kind of inclusive story. For Paul, the story of Jesus as the Christ is not just what God has done for Jesus but what God has done for all humanity. Jesus's resurrection includes the promise of resurrection for all who believe.

There is one line in this passage that has led to a difference of opinion among Christians to this day: "In the same way that everyone dies in Adam, so also everyone will be given life in Christ" (1 Cor 15:22). Notice that Paul does not say "all believers shall be made alive in Christ" but "all people." Many interpreters think he really means "all believers," which is close to what Paul sometimes says.

Other interpreters think that Paul is driven by the very story he is telling to make an even bolder claim. God is God of all. Christ is Lord of all. Everybody faces death because everybody is part of Adam's story. Everybody is promised life because everybody is part of Jesus's story.

Finally our passage makes one more christological claim. While we have seen that for Paul Jesus can be called "Lord," and that in the hymns Paul quotes it is clear that he believes the Son of God was present with God from the beginning, Paul does here make a distinction between the final authority of the Son (in traditional language) and the final authority of the Father. Christ, who in Philippians 2 receives the name above every name, nonetheless receives that name to the Glory of the Father (Phil 2:11). Here all of humankind is raised in Christ, but the final goal of everything that Christ does is again to glorify and honor God: "But when all things have been brought under his control, then the Son himself will also be under the control of the one who gave him control over everything so that God may be all in all" (or "all things for all people") (1 Cor 15:28).

Paul is not a systematic theologian; he does not explicitly ponder the question of whether the Son is subordinate to the Father, but he does insist here and elsewhere that the grand conclusion of the work of Jesus Christ is the glory of God the Father.

What about Sin? Romans 3–5

There is one other passage in his letters in which Paul reflects on the relationship between Adam and Christ. The issue now is not about death and resurrection but about sin and redemption. Paul is writing to the Romans, to churches he did not found, and he is trying to sum up his understanding of the gospel.

In brief, Paul's understanding of the gospel is that God has "justified" not only Jews, the people of the covenant, but Gentiles as well. The notion of "justification" is both rich and complicated in Paul's writings. Put as simply as I know how, Paul claims that in Jesus Christ everyone can enter into a right relationship to God. Everyone—Jew and Gentile alike—can be justified. The reason that God had to justify both Jews and Gentiles is that everybody—Jew and Gentile alike—lived in sin. The way in which God has justified both Jews and Gentiles is by sending Jesus Christ. The way that all people can receive the "justification" that God gives in Jesus Christ is by having faith in Jesus.[4]

When we talk about "sin" today, if we talk about "sin" at all, we are usually thinking of particular acts of wrongdoing: killing or gossiping or hoarding our wealth. "Sins" are sins because they are wrong. When Paul writes about sin, he is writing about the fact that every one of us does less than God intends for us. His phrase is that "all have sinned and fall short of God's glory" (Rom 3:23). Sin isn't sin just because it involves doing the wrong thing. Sin is disobedience to God and separation from God. And sin is not just the list of the wrong things we do; sin is our whole inclination to be less than God intends and our consistent tendency to turn even our most generous deeds toward selfishness.

It is hard to find a precise analogy for Paul's understanding of how deep and pervasive sin is, but some observers have helped us understand racism in America in ways that remind us of Paul's understanding of sin. Racism is not just the obvious acts of prejudice in which we engage—flying Confederate flags or using slurs for people of other ethnicities. Racism isn't even our bad thoughts about others. Racism is the deep inclination of individuals and societies to respond to others out of biases that we barely recognize or to be involved in structures that oppress others even though we are basically good-hearted people.

For Paul, sin is the deep inclination to turn from God even when we think we are turning to God and to wound other people even when we think we are helping them. It is not that everyone is terrible and depraved; it is that selfishness and disobedience creep into even our best acts.

So now that Paul has told the Romans about sin, in Romans 1–3, as a practical theologian he needs to suggest some remedy for the ailment he has diagnosed. And here is where he turns to his story of Jesus—to his Christology. Again, Paul is contrasting the story of Jesus with the story of Adam. In Genesis 2–3 Adam is disobedient, and because of his disobedience—according to the story—he is destined for death, and so are all those who come after him. Theologians since Paul have tried to decide whether sinfulness is like an hereditary disease—whether it's in our genes and there's no escaping it or whether because we are like our parents. We all turn out imitating not only their lovely qualities but also their sinfulness—all the way back to the first man and woman.

For Paul, the point is not so much the genetics of sin; it's the pervasiveness of sin. We all do disobey and fall away from the goodness of God. That is the problem. Christ is the solution, and here are the words Paul uses to describe that solution, again contrasting Jesus with Adam:

> So now the righteous requirements necessary for life are met for everyone through the righteous act of one person, just as judgment fell on everyone through the failure of one person. Many people were made

righteous through the obedience of one person, just as many were made sinners through the disobedience of one person. (Rom 5:18-19)

Jesus's one act of obedience is his death on the cross. And for Paul, Jesus's story, like Adam's story, turns out to include our story, too. Jesus died on the cross and was raised to new life. In dying on the cross Jesus reached out to all sinners to make them righteous—that is, to bring them into a close and obedient relationship to God—in rising again Jesus brought new life to all those who believed in him.

The Christology of Romans 5 is incredibly complex and subtle. After all these centuries we have a hard time imagining Christians sitting in churches in Rome listening to someone read these words from Paul and trying to pick up the heart of what he is saying. But the heart of what he is saying is something like this: Jesus's story is not Jesus's story alone. By faith Christians enter into that story. If we were left to ourselves, we would live in sin and die to nothingness. But taken up into Jesus's story, we live in obedience and die to new life. This sense that Jesus's story finally includes us all is an essential—and complicated—claim that is central to much of Paul's Christology.

And Then There Are All Those Arguments at Church: 1 Corinthians 12:12-13, 27

We notice in looking at each of the problems Paul discusses that he is writing in response to issues within communities, within churches. When Paul meditates on Jesus Christ he meditates not only on who Jesus is for the world but also on who Jesus is for the churches.[5]

This question comes to the fore in 1 Corinthians, especially in chapter 12. We have suggested that this letter to the Corinthians was written in response to information Paul had received from that congregation. Some of the information was contained in a letter; some of the information came in an oral report from "Chloe's people."

In particular, Chloe's people reported that there were divisions and disputes within the Corinthian congregation. A good part of the disagreement was around the issue of spiritual gifts. The Corinthian Christians, perhaps inspired by Paul, believed that they had received God's Holy Spirit in their baptisms. The Spirit also endowed the Corinthian believers with a variety of gifts, in the sense that we speak of someone as being "gifted" in piano or languages. On this there was apparently general agreement.

Where there was not agreement was on the relative importance of the spiritual gifts, especially the gift of speaking in tongues; the technical term is *glossalalia*. We cannot be sure exactly what the phenomenon of spiritual speech was like, but we can guess that it was not very different from speaking in tongues in churches and denominational fellowships today that are called "Pentecostal."

It is clear from 1 Corinthians 14:9-12 that to speak in tongues was to make sounds that were not ordinary human language and that in fact were by themselves unintelligible. In order to be made intelligible, they required someone to interpret them: for the Corinthians to interpret them in Greek. It also seems likely from 1 Corinthians 13:1 that those who spoke in tongues thought that they were imitating or even channeling the language of angels. So Paul reminds them, "If I speak in tongues of human beings and of angels but I don't have love, I'm a clanging gong or a clashing cymbal."

Perhaps because of their connection with the angels some of these Corinthians who had the gift of speaking in tongues thought that they were superior to those Corinthians who did not have that gift. And it may also be the case that some of the more articulate Corinthians looked down on those whose speech was sometimes unintelligible. It is certainly the case in my own denomination that the churches that include speaking in tongues in their worship sometimes think the other churches are insufficiently spiritual, while churches that do not make place for speaking in tongues sometimes think the more Pentecostal churches are simply odd.

Paul either informs or reminds the Corinthians that as members of the church they are part of the body of Christ:

> Christ is just like the human body—a body is a unit and has many parts; and all the parts of the body are one body, even though there are many. We were all baptized by one Spirit into one body, whether Jew or Greek,

or slave or free, and we all were given one Spirit to drink. You are the body of Christ and parts of each other. (1 Cor 12:12-13, 27)

These verses frame a long discussion in which Paul names some of the various spiritual gifts and compares those who have such gifts to various parts of the body. What members of the body—what Christians—cannot say to one another is, "I have no need of you." No "member" has the right to boast over another member. No member has the obligation to be ashamed of his or her unique gifts.

We are talking about who Jesus Christ is for Paul, and we notice that Paul does not say that the church is "like a body." Nor does he say that "metaphorically the church might be thought of as the body of Christ." Rather he says that the Corinthian church *is* the body of Christ. That is, he is telling the Corinthians to be who they really are: Christ's body on earth.

We can see how realistically Paul takes the claim that the church is Christ's body by looking at two other passages in 1 Corinthians.

In 1 Corinthians 6, Paul is warning Corinthian men not to have intercourse with prostitutes. His argument depends on his claim that these men really are members of the body of Christ. Therefore to join themselves with prostitutes is to join Christ with prostitutes. This is not only unwise and unhealthy and improper, but also blasphemous; it violates Christ: "Don't you know that your bodies are parts of Christ? So then, should I take parts of Christ and make them a part of someone who is sleeping around? No way!" (1 Cor 6:15).

In 1 Corinthians 11, Paul is giving instructions for the proper observance of the Lord's Supper, or the communion service, and he suggests that there are bodily consequences for the overall community and also for individual members who do not celebrate the Lord's Supper in the right way: "Those who eat and drink without correctly understanding the body are eating and drinking their own judgment. Because of this, many of you are weak and sick, and quite a few have died" (1 Cor 11:29-30). The body of Christ is present in the community but also in the meal that the community celebrates. Wrong communion has consequences for the body of the church and for the bodies within it. For Paul, therefore, part of what it means to say that Jesus is Christ and to say that Christ is risen is to say that the church, the body, represents, re-presents, embodies the risen Lord in the world.

While some theologians have wanted to say that Christ is risen only in the body of the church, that oversimplifies Paul's claim. For Paul, Christ is risen and has appeared to many believers. For Paul, Christ is present with God the Father. For Paul, Christ is not only the church's body but also the church's Lord. He is present in church and as church but also beyond church and over against church. Nonetheless we remember that for Paul church is never an optional accessory to the risen Christ or an optional home for the believers. Church is one manifestation of the claim that Christ is risen.

These are but a few of the texts in which Paul draws on his understanding of Jesus as Christ and Lord in order to address the practical problems of believers. What is striking is that what seem to be rather ordinary problems can provide the grounds for the most extraordinarily rich and consequential claims. Or perhaps what is most striking is that what seems ordinary to believers is part of a creation richer and deeper than we imagine.

This discussion reminds us that for the New Testament, Christology not only says something but also does something. Christology drives the actions necessary to solve practical problems. Christology is acted out in faith and love. Without faith and love, words about Christology become noisy gongs or clanging cymbals. If christological claims give birth to faith and love, they serve their right purpose. They feed practical theology; they shape Christian practices.

For Further Reading

Bartlett, David L. *Romans*. Louisville: Westminster John Knox, 1995.

Furnish, Victor. *Paul: Second Corinthians*. Garden City: Doubleday, 1994.

Hays, Richard B. *First Corinthians*. Louisville: Westminster John Knox, 1994.

Keck, Leander E. *Romans*. Nashville: Abingdon Press, 2005.

Proctor, John. *First and Second Corinthians*. Louisville: Westminster John Knox, 2015.

Sanders, E. P. *Paul: The Apostle's Life, Letters and Thought*. Philadelphia: Fortress, 2015.

Chapter 7
Stories Jesus Tells

In this chapter I want to look at the stories Jesus told as a way of understanding who the Gospels say Jesus was.

The first and most obvious fact to note is that all four Gospels tell us that Jesus was a storyteller. This is another way of saying what Christians and those who are not Christians have always affirmed: that Jesus was a great teacher.

Despite the efforts of many scholars through recent centuries, it is impossible to get complete consensus on which of the New Testament stories originated with the teaching of the Galilean Jesus and which may have originated in the community of believers that preached and taught in his name. Our guess is that a good many of the stories in the New Testament began with stories or sayings by Jesus but that these have been revised and adapted by the believers who passed them on over a generation or so and then further revised and adapted by the four Gospel writers who wrote the stories for their own communities. For instance in both Matthew and Luke, Jesus tells the story of the lost sheep, but the two Gospels use the parable to make very different points.

In Matthew 18:10-14, Jesus tells the story to encourage believers to seek after, discipline, and reconcile with community members who have gone astray. In Luke 15:3-7, Jesus tells the story to defend his practice of welcoming sinners and other outsiders into his fellowship. He does this in response to the criticism from the "Pharisees and legal experts" who "were grumbling, saying, 'This man welcomes sinners and eats with them'" (Luke

15:2). It is possible, of course, that Jesus used this parable on more than one occasion, but it seems more likely that the early Christians remembered the story and that Matthew and Luke each used it for his own purposes.

It is not surprising that Jesus tells stories somewhat differently in the four different Gospels. In Matthew, where Jesus seems most like a rabbi, the stories take their place in larger discourses of teaching and of biblical interpretation. In Luke, whose writer claims to be a historian—and a better writer than his predecessors—the stories have the plot and suspense we would expect from a skilled writer. In John, where Jesus speaks more often in long sermons than in short stories, the stories tend to be the starting point for the sermons. In Mark, the most puzzling of the Gospels, we are perhaps most often puzzled and perhaps even invited to puzzle.

As we look at several stories told by Jesus in the Gospels we will ask first of all what this story is doing in the context where we find it. For instance, whether or not Jesus told the three parables of Luke 15—the lost sheep, the lost coin, and the lost son—all at one time and one place we do not know. Whether the wording is exactly as he spoke it, we do not know, but that seems unlikely. We do know why Luke puts the three stories together: because they are all related to being lost and being found. We do know why he puts them in this context: they are a response to the criticism that Jesus eats with sinners and welcomes them.

In some cases we will try to guess what the parable might have been like in the setting of Jesus's own ministry, before they were revised in the telling or in the Gospel author's editing. These guesses at an original form of a story may give us some clues to the claims Jesus made about himself—even prior to his crucifixion and resurrection. In that way they are helpful for understanding the Jesus who would also be hailed as Jesus Messiah and even worshipped as Lord.

How to Read the Parables

We usually refer to the stories that Jesus tells in the Gospels as parables. This is the word Mark, our earliest Gospel, uses when Jesus begins to tell stories in chapter 4, and so this early interpreter believed that was the best word to describe Jesus's stories and has Jesus himself use the word in Mark 4:11, 13, and 30.

Moreover the word *parable* in its Greek original combines two Greek words: "to throw" and "alongside of." A parable is a story in which one word or phrase is thrown alongside another that may seem quite different. In Matthew 13, for example, the kingdom of God is compared to—thrown up against—two different men sowing seed, a mustard seed, yeast, a treasure in a field, a pearl, and a net full of fish.

The trick for the disciples and for those who read or hear the parables ever since is to understand why the kingdom can have all those images or stories thrown against it. In this way a parable works very much like a metaphor. We remember from our English classes that a metaphor takes two apparently unlike things and combines them in such a way that we have to think about their relationship. "The Lord is my shepherd" is a metaphor. "My love is a red, red rose" is another. No one hearing the first metaphor dashes out to look for the Lord carrying a shepherd's crook, and no one hearing the second thinks that the speaker has actually become infatuated with a flower.

The problem and gift of a metaphor is that no one can say what it means exactly. Psalm 23 piles metaphor upon metaphor to help us understand how the Lord is like a shepherd. The lover who says his love is like a red, red rose goes on to give us some clues of the ways in which the comparison is appropriate.

The parables are like expanded metaphors. The shortest of them is barely expanded at all: "Again, the kingdom of heaven is like a merchant in search of fine pearls. When he found one very precious pearl, he went and sold all that he owned and bought it" (Matt 13:45-46). The longest of them—like the story of the good Samaritan in Luke 10 or of the vineyard workers in Matthew 20—are long enough to be short stories. The story of the father and two sons in Luke 15:11-32 has three main characters, some minor characters, conflict, and an open ending—like a very carefully crafted work of literary art.

There are two common ways of interpreting the parables that do not value enough the way in which a parable is like a metaphor—not easily defined and depending on imagination as much as on logic. One way of interpreting the parables is to see them as being illustrations of some point that could be made just as clearly in straightforward prose. Sometimes even the Gospel writers seem to interpret the parables this way. Matthew 20:1-16 has Jesus tell the complicated story of workers who come to work at different hours and so work for different lengths of time and yet all receive exactly the same wages. At the end of the story Matthew includes a saying from Jesus that we also find elsewhere and that was probably originally not part of the story. The problem is that Matthew makes the story seem too simple by insisting that it illustrates only one point. The further problem is that the point he cites doesn't really seem to clarify the story: "So those who are last will be first. And those who are first will be last" (v. 16). Scholars and preachers ever since have tried to turn parables into illustrations of one point. The story of the merchant and the pearl of great price means: We should always be on the lookout for God's precious kingdom. Or we should always be ready to sacrifice everything we have for the sake of God's precious kingdom. Or God's kingdom really is very precious. Each of these morals, each of these attempts to tell the point of the story, makes some sense, but none even begins to tell us everything the story might tell. We shall look in a few pages at one parable to see how many nuances of interpretation we can find—as we can with a good metaphor.

Another way to interpret the parables is to see them as being allegories. An allegory is not like a metaphor, because an allegory does not leave open a range of interpretations. In an allegory we assign a spiritual meaning to every feature of the story. Every detail has a meaning outside itself, but the meaning is set and clear for the wise interpreter.

Again, we see this happening in the Gospels themselves. In Mark 4:1-9, Jesus tells the parable of a sower. Later the disciples ask what the parable means; and in Mark 4:13-20, Jesus interprets the parable as an allegory. Every feature of the story points to some spiritual truth or some moral example:

> This is the meaning of the seed that fell on the path: When the word is scattered and people hear it, right away Satan comes and steals the word

that was planted in them. Here's the meaning of the seed that fell on rocky ground: When people hear the word, they immediately receive it joyfully. Because they have no roots they last for only a little while. When they experience distress or abuse because of the word, they immediately fall away. (vv. 15-17)

Many of us who have studied this story suspect that some time after Jesus had told the original parable other Christians tried to interpret every feature of the parable as having a secret meaning. The great church fathers, early theologians, like Augustine and Origen, often took each feature of the parable as if it pointed to some spiritual truth. Most interpreters of the twentieth and twenty-first centuries try to find a clearer and more unified focus in each parable.

Parables and the Kingdom of God

Both Mark and Matthew say that Jesus began his ministry preaching about the kingdom. Mark usually calls the subject of Jesus's teaching "the kingdom of God." Perhaps because like many Jews Matthew is hesitant to speak the word *God*, Matthew writes the same phrase as "the kingdom of heaven." So in Mark's Gospel, Jesus's ministry begins with Jesus preaching: "Now is the time! Here comes God's kingdom! Change your hearts and lives, and trust this good news!" (Mark 1:15). Matthew describes the same preaching: "Change your hearts and lives! Here comes the kingdom of heaven!" (Matt 4:17).

Both Mark and Matthew include a fairly long speech during which Jesus speaks a number of parables (Mark 4; Matthew 13). Matthew has probably taken much of his material from Mark, and in each of these chapters Jesus makes clear that he is using at least some of the parables to portray the kingdom:

> Then Jesus said, "This is what God's kingdom is like. It's as though someone scatters seed on the ground, then sleeps and wakes night and day. The seed sprouts and grows." (Mark 4:26-27)

> Jesus told them another parable: "The kingdom of heaven is like someone who planted good seed in his field." (Matt 13:24)

The term translated *kingdom* can mean several related things. It can mean a geographically defined state: the kingdom of Great Britain. But it can also refer more broadly to the political powers that belong to the ruler of that state: the realm of Elizabeth II. Especially in the context of the Roman Empire, *kingdom* can represent an alternative empire—under the authority of God the Father rather than Caesar. And the word can refer to a kind of narrative, a history of activity: "This is the story of the reign of Henry VIII."

When historians and biblical scholars today write about the importance of empire in understanding either the first century or the nineteenth (or the twenty-first), they are not writing only about a geographical space or even a political arrangement but about a way of telling the story of a history where empire and imperialism is explicitly or implicitly always at work.

Notice that in the two brief introductions to parables that we just quoted the kingdom turns out to be more like a story than like either a country or a constitution. The kingdom is like the story of a man scattering seed. The kingdom is like a man who sowed seed. If we just read on in Matthew's version of these parables, for instance, we will see that the kingdom is like a mustard seed growing, like yeast multiplying, like a merchant looking, like a net being thrown. So when C. H. Dodd wrote his influential book about the parables he titled it *Parables of the Kingdom,* and he studied all Jesus's parables not just those that referred to God's kingdom explicitly.[1] All of which is to say that the kingdom is not static, does not stand still, can be better narrated than painted, is more a movie than a still photograph. For this reason we find it more helpful usually to translate the Greek terms for kingdom of God as "the reign of God," which is like the reign of Henry VIII in this way only: it can be portrayed as a drama.

We will see what that reign is like when we see how several of Jesus's parables can be read. However there is one feature of Jesus's teaching about God's reign on which there is general agreement. That reign is yet to come in all its fullness. We see stories about the triumphal climax of God's reign in Matthew 25 for example. But God's reign is also already begun. That is why we have parables like the parable of the mustard seed or the treasure in the field. That is why both Mark and Matthew have Jesus begin his preaching by saying: "The Reign is at hand" or "the Reign is near." "At hand" or "near" doesn't mean somewhere in the future. It means God's reign already has one foot in the door.

Luke's Gospel picks up something of the same theme: "Pharisees asked Jesus when God's kingdom [reign] was coming. He replied, 'God's kingdom [reign] isn't coming with signs that are easily noticed. Nor will people say, "Look, here it is!" or "There it is!"'" (Luke 17:20-21). The last part of this verse is frequently translated "the reign of God is within you," which makes Jesus's saying sound more like a matter of one's individual spiritual life. However, the original can be better translated as affirming the presence of God's reign interpersonally—among people, in the midst of human activity, even in the midst of human history.

Of course, Jesus also talks about the final appearance of the coming kingdom:

> Take care that your hearts aren't dulled by drinking parties, drunkenness, and the anxieties of day-to-day life. Don't let that day fall upon you unexpected, like a trap. It will come upon everyone who lives on the face of the whole earth. Stay alert at all times, praying that you are strong enough to escape everything that is about to happen and to stand before the Human One. (Luke 21:34-36)

For Luke, as for Paul and many other New Testament writers, the reign of God is already impinging on the present, but the day of the full appearance of God's realm is yet to come.

Some of the Stories Jesus Tells in Luke

One of the most familiar parables is the story of the good Samaritan (Luke 10:30-37). We can see the parable as the illustration of a truth. To be a neighbor is to show compassion. We can also do what some of the early church interpreters did and find in every feature of the parable a particular theological truth. Or we can try to interpret the story by looking at it as a story as Luke tells it.

Notice that Luke puts the story in the context of a story about Jesus (Luke 10:25-29). In that story Jesus acts as a teacher, a rabbi really, trying to interpret the Torah, the Law, for a seeker. A lawyer asks: "What must I do to gain eternal life?" Like many good teachers, Jesus turns the question to the questioner: "What is written in the Law?" The lawyer gives an answer that is a good summary of the heart of faithful living as defined by Jews and Christians alike, drawn from two verses in the Hebrew Bible: "*You must love the Lord your God with all your heart, with all your being, with all your strength, and with all your mind, and love your neighbor as yourself.*" Jesus commends the answer and says to the lawyer: "Do this and you will live." Presumably what Jesus means is that the lawyer will have eternal life—not only day-to-day life—since that is the kind of life the lawyer asked about.

Next, the lawyer asks a question appropriate to a lawyer. He asks about the small print, the implications, the exceptions: "And who is my neighbor?" Luke says he does this "to justify himself," which presumably means to give himself some excuse for the limits of his own neighborliness. Then comes the story:

> A man went down from Jerusalem to Jericho. He encountered thieves, who stripped him naked, beat him up, and left him near death. Now it just so happened that a priest was also going down the same road. When he saw the injured man, he crossed over to the other side of the road and went on his way. Likewise, a Levite came by that spot, saw the injured man, and crossed over to the other side of the road and went on his way. A Samaritan, who was on a journey, came to where the man was. But when he saw him, he was moved with compassion. The Samaritan went to him and bandaged his wounds, tending them with oil and wine. Then he placed the wounded man on his own donkey, took him to an inn, and took care of him. The next day, he took two full days' worth of wages and gave them to the innkeeper. He said, "Take care of him, and when I return, I will pay you back for any additional costs." (Luke 10:30-35)

For the moment we will bracket the framework of the story—the dialogue between Jesus and the lawyer—and will return to that in a few pages. As the story stands by itself we can notice some features of Jesus's call to be merciful. For one thing, the story almost certainly carried an element of shock for its first hearers. We know both from the New Testament and from other writings of the time that on the whole Jews (like those who would have heard Jesus's story) and Samaritans strongly disliked each other. To compare that time to our own, the relationship was often more like that of a zealous Israeli to a zealous Palestinian and vice versa than like that between a Presbyterian and a Methodist.

People who have studied stories among the Jews of the first centuries of our era think that the audience might have expected Jesus to include a surprise in the story, but not a big surprise. They were all set for Jesus to point out that neither of the religious leaders showed mercy on the man who was robbed and beaten. And as with stories from that day until this, once they had been shown two bad examples of human behavior, they were probably prepared that example number three would be much better. (Notice to this day how many jokes depend on three main characters: "A rabbi, a priest, and a Protestant minister went out golfing...") But while the audience would have expected that the upright character in the story would not be one of those hypocritical religious leaders, the audience most likely would have assumed that the hero would be a simple Jewish layperson, very much like themselves.

The shock was that the hero of the story turns out to be a person not like themselves at all—a Samaritan. And two surprising, nearly groundbreaking things happen in the story. First, a Samaritan is willing to stop and help a Jew. Second, a Jew is willing to receive help from a Samaritan. Furthermore, the story reflects a reality that has haunted any attempt to be neighborly from the first century until now. Notice how easily and quickly Jesus can talk about the priest and the Levite. The priest looked, crossed the road, and passed by on the other side. No time at all; very little effort. A short sentence describes a moral shortcoming. The description of the Levite is almost exactly the same. The description of the Samaritan's response is far more elaborate.

> But the Samaritan,
> Saw him
> Was moved with pity
> Went to him
> Bandaged his wounds

Poured oil and wine on them
Put him on his animal
Brought him to an inn
Took care of him there
Paid the innkeeper for further care
Promised to stop back and pay off any remaining costs.

When someone faces an opportunity for kindness and says "I can't be bothered," the disclaimer gets it exactly right. Neighborliness is a bother; neighborliness takes bother. The story demonstrates something that rings entirely true: the simplicity of apathy and the complexity of compassion.

The story also shows a theme frequently found in Jesus's teaching. The officially religious are often not actually faithful. Time after time when Jesus criticizes the religious leaders of his community it is not because they teach wrongly; it is because they do not live out their own teachings.

Finally, in the larger context of Luke's Gospel, notice how Luke shapes or recalls Jesus's conversation with the lawyer. The lawyer has opened the way for a parable by asking Jesus to answer his question: "Who is my neighbor?" Jesus never answers that question at all; he turns it entirely around and says: "Go be a neighbor."

> "What do you think? Which one of these three was a neighbor to the man who encountered thieves?" Then the legal expert said, "The one who demonstrated mercy toward him." Jesus told him, "Go and do likewise." (Luke 10:36-37)

Here are some facts we learn about Jesus the storyteller when we hear his story. First, he knows that his message is often best conveyed through stories. He is perfectly capable of giving commands or interpreting texts, but sometimes he tells a story. If, as we have seen, his preaching is often about God as ruler, maybe it is better to talk about God's reign—which can be the focus of a story—than God's kingdom, which sounds like a place we could trace on a map.

Second, Jesus is at ease with his own authority. Of course by the time the Gospels are written, Christians are entirely convinced that Jesus speaks truth and has every right to do so. But the stories themselves, insofar as we can trace them back to Jesus's own ministry, are often remarkable in their claim to know what God is doing and their willingness to show us a picture of that action. And likewise Jesus claims remarkable authority in his willingness to show believers what a faithful response looks like. His parables never end with, "On the other hand, you might not need to be neighborly at all; that's just one option."

Third, in the parables long enough to be short stories, Jesus is acutely aware of the way the world really works. We are strikingly short on fables illustrated with talking animals or narratives set in a galaxy far away or a time long ago. Life gets difficult for the Samaritan because neighborliness is difficult. In another famous parable, the older brother gets jealous because that's what people do (Luke 15:11-32); and in another story, workers who have been laboring in a vineyard all day are incredibly angry when they get the same wages as the latecomers who wandered in only an hour before sunset (Matt 20:1-16).

Fourth, the stories are often not only recognizably human but also surprisingly surprising. The Samaritan surprises us. The father who holds no grudges against either son surprises us. The vineyard owner who gives just as generously to the late workers as to the early would flunk any course at business school then or now. The stories show us things as we expect, and then they twist our expectations. Perhaps for Jesus, the story of God's reign is a story of twisted expectations.

The other most familiar parable is the story we usually call the prodigal son, though it is really the story of two sons and their relationship to their father (Luke 15:11-32). In looking at the story of the good Samaritan I suggested that it was probably Luke who gave this parable its narrative framework—the dialogue between Jesus and the lawyer. I think it is also likely that Luke provided the setting for the story of the father and the sons and that it is he who brought together the three parables of the lost sheep, the lost coin, and the lost young man. At the end of our discussion of this parable we shall say a word about how Luke interprets the story. But we can begin by trying to take the story in itself:

> Jesus said, "A certain man had two sons. The younger son said to this father, 'Father, give me my share of the inheritance.' Then the father

divided his estate between them. Soon afterward, the younger son gathered everything together and took a trip to a land far away. There, he wasted his wealth through extravagant living.

When he had used up his resources, a severe food shortage arose in that country and he began to be in need. He hired himself out to one of the citizens of that country, who sent him into his fields to feed pigs. He longed to eat his fill from what the pigs ate, but no one gave him anything. When he came to his senses, he said, 'How many of my father's hired hands have more than enough food, but I'm starving to death! I will get up and go to my father, and say to him, "Father, I have sinned against heaven and against you. I no longer deserve to be called your son. Take me on as one of your hired hands."' So he got up and went to his father.

While he was still a long way off, his father saw him and was moved with compassion. His father ran to him, hugged him, and kissed him. Then his son said, 'Father, I have sinned against heaven and against you. I no longer deserve to be called your son.' But the father said to his servants, 'Quickly, bring out the best robe and put it on him! Put a ring on his finger and sandals on his feet! Fetch the fattened calf and slaughter it. We must celebrate with feasting because this son of mine was dead and has come back to life! He was lost and is found!' And they began to celebrate.

Now his older son was in the field. Coming in from the field, he approached the house and heard music and dancing. He called one of the servants and asked what was going on. The servant replied, 'Your brother has arrived, and your father has slaughtered the fattened calf because he received his son back safe and sound.' Then the older son was furious and didn't want to enter in, but his father came out and begged him. He answered his father, 'Look, I've served you all these years, and I never disobeyed your instruction. Yet you've never given me as much as a young goat so I could celebrate with my friends. But when this son of yours returned, after gobbling up your estate on prostitutes, you slaughtered the fattened calf for him.' Then his father said, 'Son, you are always with me, and everything I have is yours. But we had to celebrate and be glad because this brother of yours was dead and is alive. He was lost and is found.'"

What strikes us first about this parable is that it is a fully developed short story with two contrasting sections and three fully developed characters. We traditionally call this the parable of the prodigal son, but it might equally well be called the story of the two brothers or the story of the loving father. Jesus does not tell us who every character in the story represents: the father is not exactly God; the younger son is not exactly sinful humankind; the elder son is not exactly prideful humankind. However, like a metaphor, the story sheds light on the world of faith and faithlessness and helps those who hear it or read it think about who this God is whom Jesus preaches and whom he represents.

Notice a few features of the overall story:

- The two sons get almost equal treatment in terms of the amount of space and attention given to their stories.
- They also get (almost) equal treatment from the father. He reaches out to each of them, to the younger son as he comes home from the far country and to the older son as he comes in from the field.
- The story remains entirely open-ended. The story ends with the invitation of the father to the older son to come to the party and to welcome the younger son home, but we will never know whether the elder son accepts the invitation. In this way the story remains an invitation for those who heard it in the first century and those who hear it today: how do we respond to the invitation to be reconciled with our brothers and sisters?

We notice some particular details of the first part of the story. Scholars disagree on the exact details of inheritance laws in Jesus's world and in Luke's, but it seems quite clear that the younger son acts presumptuously and perhaps scandalously in asking to take his share of his father's goods while his father is still alive. By implication he acts as if he wishes his father were dead.

The story traces the son's self-destruction. First he wastes everything he has received. Then he takes an unpleasant job made worse by the fact that he spends his time with pigs, an animal that his religion has designated as unclean, not to be eaten by the faithful. He comes to recognize the sadness of his situation only when he is in the most reduced circumstances. Some have thought that the son shows how self-centered he is when he repents only because of an empty stomach. Some are more inclined to think that our wills are often related to our stomachs and our self-awareness to our loss of comfort.

Notice that while the son is prepared to give his speech of repentance, his father sees him a long way off and welcomes him home before he can even stammer out his carefully prepared speech. However indirectly, this part of the story shows us something of what Jesus thinks about the nature of the God he preaches. That God goes seeking those who have turned away from God. That God is in the business of welcoming. And however indirectly, this part of the story shows us something of who Jesus thinks we are as humans. We are those who insist on our own way sometimes to our own detriment. We are those who are called to take a good look at ourselves. If we are trying to understand who Jesus is in Luke's Gospel we can see that he is the one who represents that welcoming and forgiving God. And we can also see that he holds up a mirror to our own lives, so that like the younger son we can come to ourselves.

In the second part of the story, notice that the father does not for a minute distance himself from the elder son: "Son, you are always with me, and everything I have is yours." What the father does do is to seek to bridge the gap between the older brother and the younger. The older brother refuses to acknowledge his own relationship to the prodigal: "But when this son of yours returned, after gobbling up your estate on prostitutes." The father tries to call his son back from distancing himself: "This brother of yours was dead and is alive." The distancing may include the accusation that the younger brother spent time with prostitutes; we have only the angry brother's word for this.

The parable tells two stories about distance—the distance of the far country and the distance of the field just out the door. It tells the story of the distance of son from father and of brother from brother. It seems likely that when Jesus first told this story he was talking about God's reign as that drama in which those who have felt far from God are brought home to God's care and those who have alienated themselves from their brothers and sisters are invited to come home to the family celebration.

In the context of Luke's Gospel, the story suggests two further implications, or hints at two other insights. First, the story and the two stories that precede it are inspired by a complaint about Jesus. He welcomes tax collectors and sinners. Those who accuse him are the religious leaders of their community. In Luke's story we can assume that they are more like the older brother than like the younger and that the sinners and tax collectors (who were unpopular not just because nobody likes taxes but because they often collaborated with the occupying empire) are like the younger brother—in their own kind of far country. So when Jesus invites these prodigals to eat with him he is himself enacting the banquet of the parable, and by implication telling the scribes and Pharisees that they are also welcome at the party if they will just have the good grace to come in. Since this is a book about who Jesus is in the New Testament, we note that here Jesus embodies the story he tells. He reconciles people to God and to each other.

Second, the story of the two brothers is the third of three stories—the story of the wayward sheep (15:3-7), the story of the missing coin (15:8-10), and the story of the runaway son (15:11-32). Each of these stories is about something precious that is lost and then found again. Each of these stories is about the call to rejoice in the finding. The scribes and Pharisees set the context for the three stories: "This man welcomes sinners and eats with them" (15:2). For Luke, Jesus is this man who will risk everything to find a sheep that went astray. Jesus is the man who will turn the house upside down to find just one coin. Jesus is the man who welcomes home missing children and reunites alienated siblings. And while for Luke it is probably not the case that Jesus is God in the flesh, it is very much the case that Jesus does God's work, embodies God's reign.

Some of the Stories Jesus Tells in Matthew

In Matthew's Gospel Jesus tells another story about unexpected generosity and unsurprising resentment.

> [Jesus said] The kingdom of heaven is like a landowner who went out early in the morning to hire workers for his vineyard. After he agreed with the workers to pay them a denarion, he sent them into his vineyard.
> Then he went out around nine in the morning and saw others standing around the marketplace doing nothing. He said to them, "You also

go into the vineyard, and I'll pay you whatever is right." And they went.

Again around noon and then at three in the afternoon, he did the same thing. Around five in the afternoon he went and found others standing around, and he said to them, "Why are you just standing around here doing nothing all day long?"

"Because nobody has hired us," they replied.

He responded, "You also go into the vineyard."

When evening came, the owner of the vineyard said to his manager, "Call the workers and give them their wages, beginning with the last ones hired and moving on finally to the first." When those who were hired at five in the afternoon came, each one received a denarion. Now when those hired first came, they thought they would receive more. But each of them also received a denarion. When they received it, they grumbled against the landowner, "These who were hired last worked one hour, and they received the same pay as we did even though we had to work the whole day in the hot sun."

But he replied to one of them, "Friend, I did you no wrong. Didn't I agree to pay you a denarion? Take what belongs to you and go. I want to give to this one who was hired last the same as I give to you. Don't I have the right to do what I want with what belongs to me? Or are you resentful because I'm generous?" So those who are last will be first. And those who are first will be last. (Matt 20:1-16)

It seems likely that Matthew as author and editor has added the first and last verse of this story. As with so many of Jesus's parables, Matthew believes this parable reveals something of the kingdom of God. We have suggested that the "reign of God" may be a better translation of Matthew's phrase here because the reign of God suggests God's activity, and the parable is an account of action—the action of the landowner and the action of the workers.

The last verse, "So those who are last will be first. And those who are first will be last," is a saying attributed to Jesus that occurs at various places in the Gospels and probably was not originally attached to this parable. The saying does, however, let us see Matthew's perspective on the parable. In the story of God's reign we see a story of those who come last being treated just the same as those who come first. Matthew probably tells the story especially to insist to his audience that Gentiles have as much right to be part of God's story as Jews do. Although Jews have had the law and the promises of God for centuries and have worked hard in the vineyard, even those who have come at the last minute—the Gentiles—receive the same rights and privileges as those who work all day.

Several features of the story are striking. First, this is not finally a story about what is fair. Whatever the story is about, it is not about equal work for equal pay; it is probably not finally about pay at all, but it is a metaphor, a picture of a different kind of economy. Second, the dilemma of the workers is portrayed entirely from the perspective of the workers who have been in the vineyard all day. When they see the generous wages given the latecomers, it is not that they immediately object to the master's generosity; it is that they expect to receive even more generous rewards. Third, the landowner does not lie to anyone. He gives each person what he promised. Objectively speaking, he does not go back on his word. And, finally, it is clear that the landowner claims to be answerable only to himself and his own generosity: "Don't I have the right to do what I want with what belongs to me? Or are you resentful because I am generous?" (The Greek of the Gospel is a little more puzzling: "Is your eye evil because I am good?" The implication of the idiom is that the grumblers are envious or jealous.)

All these features cause the listener to suspect that this is not a story about right economics but about some other kind of calculation. Whatever it is that the landowner gives, it is the landowner who gets to decide the amount to be given. However hard it is that the early laborers have worked, they should not grumble when they get only what is promised.

Surely what is at stake here is not money but membership in God's reign. God's reign makes room for those who have worked long (for people who have worked from Moses on, or for Christians who have been in church all their lives). God's reign makes room for those who have only come recently to the vineyard—for the Gentiles or for that notorious sinner Uncle Charlie who only came to faith in the last weeks of his life.

In the context of Matthew's Gospel there is little question that this has become a story of God's grace and how it brings blessing and conflict alike.[2] *Grace*, a New Testament word for God's generous and loving goodness, is not given out in different amounts depending on how worthy or how hardworking the recipient may be. Grace is entirely God's gift and depends entirely on God's promise to provide that grace for longtime believers and for brand new believers alike.

That is how I read the story in Matthew. And Jesus the storyteller represents the one who upsets our standard expectations about what is fair, helps us to understand how to receive what is generous. He is also the one in whom that generosity is manifest. As we have already suggested that Jesus is himself God's parable, in this context we discover that Jesus is himself God's gift provided for those who work all day and for those who sneak in just before the closing bell.

At least one scholar has suggested that in Jesus's own ministry—before Matthew wrote his Gospel and before the church was underway—this was more a story about God's justice than about God's mercy. According to William Herzog this story was originally told in a setting in which workers were regularly exploited by landowners.[3] As Jesus originally told the story, listeners were not invited to agree with the landowner's claim to justice but to agree with those who had worked far longer than other workers yet who received the same pay. The parable calls the exploited farm laborers of Jesus's time to gather in protest against the unfairness of their plight. Insofar as this is a parable about God's reign, it is a call to work toward the fulfillment of that reign where economic fairness will be a reality for all.

We have said that parables are so rich that they cannot be reduced to any one meaning or mined for only one application. In the context of Matthew's Gospel it seems quite clear that this story is a story about God's keeping God's promises even when those promises may offend our sense of fairness.

Herzog is in some ways a forerunner of the post-colonial theorists who have found in the New Testament strong signs of resistance to the economic and political rule of Rome and of Rome's clients in the colonies. It may be that in his ministry Jesus told a version of this story to stir up opposition to economic injustice. Insofar as this book is a study about the Christology of the New Testament rather than the claims of "the historical" Jesus, we can say that for Matthew the landowner of this parable like the father in Luke's parable of the prodigal is marked by a generosity toward outsiders, latecomers, and Gentiles that would understandably be annoying to insiders, lifelong believers, and faithful Jews.

In another long story, later in his Gospel, Matthew does have Jesus address quite explicitly the situation of the oppressed and the marginalized.

Now when the Human One [literally, "Son of Man"] comes in his majesty and all his angels are with him, he will sit on his majestic throne. All the nations will be gathered in front of him. He will separate them from each other, just as a shepherd separates the sheep from the goats. He will put the sheep on his right side. But the goats he will put on his left.

Then the king will say to those on his right, "Come, you who will receive good things from my Father. Inherit the kingdom that was prepared for you before the world began. I was hungry and you gave me food to eat. I was thirsty and you gave me a drink. I was a stranger and you welcomed me. I was naked and you gave me clothes to wear. I was sick and you took care of me. I was in prison and you visited me."

Then those who are righteous will reply to him, "Lord, when did we see you hungry and feed you, or thirsty and give you a drink? When did we see you as a stranger and welcome you, or naked and give you clothes to wear? When did we see you sick or in prison and visit you?"

Then the king will reply to them, "I assure you that when you have done it for one of the least of these brothers and sisters of mine, you have done it for me."

Then he will say to those on his left, "Get away from me, you who will receive terrible things. Go into the unending fire that has been prepared for the devil and his angels. I was hungry and you didn't give me food to eat. I was thirsty and you didn't give me anything to drink. I was a stranger and you didn't welcome me. I was naked and you didn't give me clothes to wear. I was sick and in prison, and you didn't visit me."

Then they will reply, "Lord, when did we see you hungry or thirsty or a stranger or naked or sick or in prison and didn't do anything to help you?" Then he will answer, "I assure you that when you haven't done it for one of the least of these, you haven't done it for me." And they will go away into eternal punishment. But the righteous ones will go into eternal life. (Matt 25:31-46)

It is obvious that here in Matthew Jesus tells a relatively long story, but it is also clear that for Matthew this story is not a parable. In Matthew's Gospel this is the fourth story that Jesus tells as part of the same speech. Each of the two preceding stories begins with a reminder that this is a parable, a metaphor:

> At that time the kingdom of heaven will be like ten young bridesmaids who took their lamps. (Matt 25:1)

> The kingdom of heaven is like a man who was leaving on a trip. He called his servants. (Matt 25:14)

When Jesus begins this speech, however, there is no mark that this is a comparison; this story is not a metaphor, not a simile, not a parable. The story presents a straightforward description: "When the Son of Man comes in his glory..." To be sure the description is of something yet to come, more like a vision perhaps than a report. To be sure the whole description depends on an implicit simile: some Christians will be like sheep, some like goats.

The heart of the story seems fairly clear. At the judgment day people will be judged not by the orthodoxy of their doctrine but by the depth of their compassion. It is far less clear whether as Matthew tells the story of the judgment of the nations he is reminding his fellow Christians that they are called to compassion or whether he is assuring them that those powerful people among whom they live will be judged by their generosity to the struggling Christians.[4]

For purposes of contemporary understanding the point becomes very much the same. The storyteller and teacher here tell and teach that faithfulness to him requires compassion and generosity for those who are in need.

Notice three features of this story.

First, those who encounter Christ among the naked, hungry, thirsty, and imprisoned are surprised to find him there. They fulfill their obligation as obligation and are delighted to discover that the obligation brings blessing as well. Or they ignore their obligations and are astonished to learn that apathy brings harsh judgment. Second, the whole story presupposes the resurrection of Jesus. For the community that hears Matthew's Gospel Jesus is alive because he is the king who will judge the nations. He is alive because he is present in the suffering and alienation of those who are distressed and oppressed. We are far here from the later claim that Jesus Christ is entirely God and entirely human, but we have a vision of Jesus as immeasurably powerful and immediately vulnerable that points toward that later more systematic claim. Third, the same Jesus whom we have seen as teacher and healer, the same Jesus who will soon be crucified and raised from the empty tomb, will return at the end of history as the judge of all the world; all the nations will be gathered before *him* (25:32).[5]

It is perhaps here clearest of all that the storyteller embodies the stories he tells. Like the Samaritan he reaches out across lines of race, religion, and ethnicity. Like the Father he welcomes those who have gone far away and urges those who have stayed near to be reconciled to their brothers and sisters. Like the landowner he is the giver of equal grace and kindness to all, and he is himself that gift. As the king he judges human compassion, and as the sufferer he receives it.

Finally the Gospel writers give their own answer to Jesus's question: "To what shall we compare the reign of God?" The answer is, "to Jesus himself."

For Further Reading

Dodd, C. H. *Parables of the Kingdom.* New York: Scribner's, 1961.

Herzog, William R. *Parables as Subversive Speech.* Louisville: Westminster John Knox, 1996.

Jeremias, Joachim. *The Parables of Jesus.* Translated by S. H. Hooke. New York: Scribner's, 1972.

Levine, Amy-Jill. *Short Stories by Jesus: The Enigmatic Parables of a Controversial Rabbi.* New York: Harper One, 2015.

Perrin, Norman. *Jesus and the Language of the Kingdom.* Philadelphia: Fortress, 1976.

Robinson, Marilynne. *The Givenness of Things.* New York: Farrar, Strauss and Giroux, 2015.

Chapter 8

Stories about Jesus: The Gospels (Mark and Matthew)

Not only did Jesus tell stories that help us understand him and his mission, but also he was the subject of a number of stories. There are four fairly long accounts of Jesus's story in the New Testament, which are the four Gospels: Matthew, Mark, Luke, and John. There are also a number of other books called gospels in the early centuries of the Common Era. Most of them are later than the four Gospels of the New Testament. The one that is fairly early—the Gospel of Thomas—consists mostly of sayings.

Three of the Gospels—Matthew, Mark, and Luke—are called the Synoptic Gospels because they follow very much the same outline, or synopsis. The Gospel of John has many features in common with the other three Gospels, but it is quite different in its plot and very different in the picture it gives both of Jesus's teaching and of his final days.

There is general but not universal agreement that Mark was the earliest of the Gospels and that Matthew and Luke followed Mark's outline. Indeed, they used much of Mark's words in writing their own Gospels.

Both Matthew and Luke have stories and sayings that belong to that Gospel alone—like the parable of the prodigal son in Luke 15:11-32 and the story of the workers in the vineyard in Matthew 20:1-16. Matthew and Luke also have a number of passages in common that are not taken from Mark. Many students of the Gospel think that they had a common source. We call that source "Q" (from the German word *quelle*, which means "source"). We don't have any copies of "Q"; we make our best guesses about what it contained by comparing Matthew and Luke.

We do not know anything about the authors of the Gospels apart from the books that they wrote, and even their names are guesses made by the early copiers of their works.

Though we can be fairly sure that Mark is the earliest Gospel, we are not sure of the order in which the other Gospels were written. My best guess is that the order of writing was Mark, then Matthew, then Luke, then John. In any case we shall look at the four long narratives about Jesus in that order—Mark and Matthew in this chapter and Luke and John in the next.

In discussing the different stories told by the four Gospels it may be helpful to characterize each of them by comparison to a kind of literature that is familiar to us from our larger culture. Mark is much like a tragedy (with a surprise ending). Matthew is a guidebook. Luke is explicitly writing a history. John writes a kind of trial novel, with witnesses and testimony and a verdict.

Mark: The Gospel as (Almost) Tragedy

Mark made one of the most significant decisions in the development of early Christology. Paul, who wrote earlier than Mark, included many claims about Jesus, but apart from a few words about the last supper (in 1 Corinthians 11) and about Jesus's resurrection (in 1 Corinthians 15) he did not really tell any stories about Jesus or even often quote Jesus's sayings. When Mark wrote his Gospel the first disciples and other Christian preachers and teachers had certainly told stories about Jesus and quoted sayings and parables attributed to him. Some of these sayings and stories may even have been written down in collections for the use of other preachers and teachers; we do not know. Christian communities had sung hymns about Jesus and even hymns to Jesus, and their songs implied an understanding of who Jesus was.

We are, however, quite sure that Mark was the first person to write down the story of Jesus from the beginning of his ministry through the discovery of the empty tomb. When Mark did this he made a claim that has been central to Christology ever since: one way to understand Jesus is to understand him as the hero or protagonist of a story. We can know who Jesus Christ is for Mark (and for the other Gospels) by trying to understand the story—the characters, the plot, the settings—rather as we might try to understand a short novel today. Since the last part of the twentieth century a number of scholars have suggested that one way to understand the Gospels is to see how they function as stories—much as one might try to understand a story by Alice Munro or William Trevor who are two modern masters of shorter fiction. This is not to say that Jesus or Peter or Mary are fictional characters, but that they function in the Gospels as characters do in other kinds of narrative literature. The critics who study the Gospels from this perspective are known as "literary critics," though as in other kinds of literary criticism they represent a number of rather distinct approaches to their work.

In his later writings the scholar Jack Dean Kingsbury approached the Gospels as works of literature. He pointed out that we can see in Mark's Gospel many of the features of a good story—most obviously in the presentation of characters and in the development of a plot.[1]

When we study the characters in Mark's Gospel we notice immediately that Jesus is the hero or protagonist of the story and that his place in the story is developed far more fully than that of any other character. In fact the whole point of the story is to let the reader understand who Jesus was and for Christian believers to understand who he still is. As readers of more recent stories we also notice that Mark tells us almost nothing about Jesus's interior life. We are used to long descriptions of what a hero is thinking and how he or she is feeling, but Mark gives us very little of that. For the most part we see Jesus from a public perspective. We see what he did; we hear what he said. Occasionally, as at the Garden of Gethsemane, we come closer to a description of Jesus's interior life, but those moments in this Gospel are rare.

There is also a supporting cast of characters. John the Baptizer helps introduce the story. The disciples—especially Andrew, James, and John and most especially Peter—figure prominently in the story, and it may be that the readers are most supposed to identify with them.

Furthermore, there are women followers who appear especially toward the end of the story and whose names are still remembered in the community: two Marys and Salome, who appear both at the foot of the cross and at the door of the tomb. Mark further tells us that these women had accompanied Jesus throughout all his ministry in Galilee (Mark 15:40-41).

Some of Jesus's opponents are also named: Pilate, Caiaphas, and Judas. But there are also more general categories of opponents: scribes and Pharisees.

Many of the characters in the story are not named and enter the story only for one scene; in fact, people needing to be healed are especially prominent in this Gospel. Quite often we notice that they come to faith more fully than the named characters do. The only minor characters to get named are Bartimaeus and Simon of Cyrene; we can guess that Mark's readers may have known of them or their families (see Mark 10:46 and 15:21).

Finally there are two characters who are not human: Satan and God. Satan gets only a brief scene when he tempts Jesus in the wilderness (Mark 1:13). God speaks at two key moments: Jesus's baptism (Mark 1:11) and the scene on the mountain where Jesus is changed, transfigured, in the presence of the disciples (Mark 9:7).

And the narrator of the story, while he is not a character exactly, figures prominently in the telling.

God, Jesus, and the narrator are all entirely reliable; we can believe what they tell us. Jesus's opponents are consistently unreliable; they say the wrong thing or they say the right thing for the wrong reason.

The unnamed people who get healed are reliable examples of faith.

The disciples, it seems, are caught between confusion and understanding.

The plot of Mark's story can be fairly easily sketched. The story begins in Galilee, which is Jesus's home territory. Jesus begins his ministry with his baptism. He gathers disciples to share in ministry with him. He engages in healings and preaches parables. He enters disputes with his opponents, the scribes, the Pharisees, and in one case another group of Jewish leaders, the Sadducees. Two-thirds of the way through the Gospel Jesus enters the city of Jerusalem. There he engages in troublemaking at the temple, which was the heart of Jewish piety and a sign of stability in the Roman colony of Judea. He gives a long speech predicting the end of history. He is betrayed to the authorities by Judas Iscariot, one of his disciples, arrested, tried, and executed on a cross. He is buried, but on the third day the women who come to embalm him discover that the tomb is empty.

Even this brief description of the plot indicates that our story is the story of an extraordinary person and that his life is bounded and directed by what Mark understands as the purposes of God. The story focuses on the goodness of that person, the hero, Jesus. As in a tragedy the hero's very strengths become his liabilities when they threaten others. Jesus's faithfulness to God is a threat both to the religious authorities who oppose him and to the Roman authorities who finally crucify him.

If the story ended with Mark 15:39, it would end as many tragedies end, with the death of the hero and the recognition that the most worthy character in the drama has died. At the end of Shakespeare's tragedy *Hamlet*, a soldier who had stood outside the drama till then, Fortinbras, offers the words of recognition:

> *Let four captains*
> *Bear Hamlet, like a soldier, to the stage;*
> *For he was likely, had he been put on,*
> *To have proved most royally.*[2]

At the end of Mark's tragedy (or almost tragedy) an unnamed centurion who had stood outside the drama till then offers the words of recognition: "This man was certainly God's Son" (Mark 15:39).

Yet Mark's Gospel is not quite a classic tragedy. It does not end with the death of the hero and his acclamation by an observer. There is one more scene, involving a burial and an empty tomb. They are presented so briefly that they may seem not to outweigh or even balance the loss they are meant to reverse. Jan Hagens, a lecturer in comparative literature at Yale University, notes that Mark is in some ways more like one of Shakespeare's so-called romances, plays in which the hero or heroine undergoes enormous testing and loss and seems to be entirely defeated. But then there is a final scene, almost too abrupt, that tries to show that good can triumph even over five acts of sorrow and loss.[3]

In Shakespeare's play *Cymbeline*, the king of Britain, Cymbeline, believes that his daughter Imogen is dead. If not exactly through mystery or magic, through cunning and confusion at the end of the play, his daughter is restored to the father's presence, and Cymbeline closes the play with a word of thanks and blessing, not only of his reconciliation with his daughter, but of the hope for reconciliation between warring nations.

> *Laud we the gods;*
> *And let our crooked smokes climb to their nostrils*
> *From our blest altars. Publish we this peace*
> *To all our subjects. Set we forward; let*
> *A Roman and a British ensign wave*
> *Friendly together.*[4]

In the even more complicated plot of Shakespeare's *The Winter's Tale*, King Leontes is sure that his wife is dead until she is restored to him by events that are almost miraculous—almost a resurrection. Leontes is not struck dumb with amazement (as are the women in Mark), but he is amazed:

> *Thou hast found [my wife]*
> *But how, is to be questioned; for I saw her*
> *As I thought, dead, and have in vain said many*
> *A prayer upon her grave.*[5]

In Mark, as well, the fifteen chapters of courage, opposition, and finally death are surprisingly reversed by eight verses of hope, including the young man's announcement: "You are looking for Jesus of Nazareth, who was crucified. He has been raised. He isn't here" (Mark 16:6).

We can look at a few details of Mark's Gospel story better to understand who Jesus is in Mark's story and what it means for Mark to say in his first line that Jesus is Messiah. (Mark probably also says here that Jesus is Son of God, though some early manuscripts leave that out.)

(Almost) the Beginning, the Middle, and (Almost) the End

At the beginning of the twentieth century a German scholar named William Wrede said that Mark's Gospel was notable for the frequent occurrence of what he called "the messianic secret."[6] Time after time Jesus will perform a miracle and tell the disciples to keep it quiet; or he will heal someone who is not to reveal the healing; or he will even appear in heaven with Moses and Elijah but insist that no one tell.

We shall look again at the motif of secrecy in this Gospel and suggest what it says about Mark's Christology. But for now we note that the heart of Mark's Gospel is not so much the proclamation that Jesus is the Messiah, the anointed one (though he is clearly that). The heart of Mark's Gospel is that Jesus is the Son of God.

We know that this is the heart of the Gospel because it is God who says so, once toward the beginning of the book and once at the middle.

In the story of Jesus's baptism we have this description:

> About that time, Jesus came from Nazareth of Galilee, and John baptized him in the Jordan River. While he was coming up out of the water, Jesus saw heaven splitting open and the Spirit, like a dove, coming down on him. And there was a voice from heaven: "You are my Son, whom I dearly love; in you I find happiness. (Mark 1:9-11)

Especially when we compare this story with the Gospels of Matthew and Luke we notice two striking features of the story.

First, this is the first time in the story that Mark claims that Jesus is Son of God. Both Matthew and Luke include long sections in their Gospels that indicate that Jesus is Son of God and of the virgin Mary, from the beginning of his life. Here it may be that Jesus actually is adopted, declared as Son of God at his baptism. Mark's account of God's word to Jesus echoes Psalm 2:7: "You are my son, today I have become your father." Before long the official teaching of most churches will be that Jesus was Son of God from the beginning of his ministry, or perhaps even from the beginning of time. In Mark, it may be that he becomes God's son as his ministry begins, at his baptism.

Second, only in Mark's Gospel are the words of God spoken to Jesus alone: "You are my son" (1:11 NRSV). There is no indication that anyone other than Jesus hears these words, and in this way the great secret of the Gospel is a secret so far shared by no one else within the story itself. The author knows who Jesus is. The reader knows who Jesus is (especially if "Son of God" was included in Mark 1:1), but no human character has yet heard Jesus's sonship declared.

In the middle of the story it is still God who declares Jesus to be God's son, but now at last there are human witnesses. Peter, James, and John go with Jesus to the top of the mountain. They see the vision of Jesus, shining bright as the sun, talking with Moses and Elijah. And they hear God's affirmation: "This is my Son, whom I dearly love. Listen to him!" (Mark 9:7). But now though these three disciples know the secret of Jesus's sonship, they are told to keep it secret until after Jesus's resurrection (Mark 9:9).

Now it happens in the world of Mark's Gospel that by the time we get to chapter 9 only God and the author have proclaimed Jesus to be son of God, and though no human character in the story has known who Jesus is, the demons recognize his sonship rather clearly (see Mark 3:11; 5:7).

At almost the end of the Gospel is the story of Jesus's crucifixion, and now for the first time it is one of the human characters in the story who proclaims what for Mark is a central truth: "When the centurion, who stood facing Jesus, saw how he died, he said, 'This man was certainly God's Son'" (Mark 15:39).[7]

In Mark's Gospel, as in Matthew's, Jesus's last words before his death are: "My God, my God, why have you left me?" (Mark 15:34). These are not only Jesus's last words but also the first words of Psalm 22, and some students of this text think that Jesus is referring to the whole psalm, which starts with despair but moves toward hope.

However, we can be quite sure that what the centurion heard was just the one sentence: "My God, my God, why have you left me?" and in the world of our story it seems highly unlikely that he was supposed to have the larger context of Psalm 22 at hand. The centurion has seen mockery; he has seen torture, and he has heard the cry of abandonment. And then with all that before him he says: "This man was certainly God's Son."

What comes clear is that Mark, in showing the narrative of Jesus, claims that the fact that Jesus suffers and dies is part of what it means for him to be Son of God. In different ways both Matthew and Luke will soften this claim. But any understanding of Christology in Mark has to notice that Jesus is Son of God, not despite the fact that he suffers, but because of the fact that he suffers.

The Very Beginning and the Very End

The first words of Mark's Gospel are: "The beginning of the good news [or gospel] about Jesus, God's Son" (Mark 1:1). We have suggested that "the beginning of the good news" may be the title that Mark gives to his entire book. For him there is not yet a set genre of literature called "a Gospel" so that he may not know that the whole of his book will be called a Gospel. He may want to name his book "the beginning of the Gospel." If this is the case we are bound to ask where the Gospel goes next, after we have finished hearing the story contained in Mark 1:1–16:8.

A possible answer to this question might be found in the ending of Mark's book. Some translations of the Bible include Mark 16:9-20, which has several appearances by the risen Jesus, a commissioning of the disciples to continue Jesus's ministry, and the story of the risen Jesus's ascension into heaven. However, the earliest copies we have of Mark's book end with Mark 16:8. The material from Mark 16:9-20 seems to have been added in later manuscripts and in fact it reads like a kind of patchwork of material from the other three Gospels augmented by some novel features like the promise about snake handling.

The earliest manuscripts we have of the Gospel of Mark end like this:

> When the Sabbath was over, Mary Magdalene, Mary the mother of James, and Salome bought spices so that they could go and anoint Jesus' dead body. Very early on the first day of the week, just after sunrise, they came to the tomb. They were saying to each other, "Who's going to roll the stone away from the entrance for us?" When they looked up, they saw that the stone had been rolled back. (And it was a very large stone!) Going into the tomb, they saw a young man in a white robe seated on the right side; and they were startled. But he said to them, "Don't be alarmed! You are looking for Jesus of Nazareth, who was crucified. He has been raised. He isn't here. Look, here's the place where they laid him. Go, tell his disciples, especially Peter, that he is going ahead of you into Galilee. You will see him there, just as he told you." Overcome with terror and dread, they fled from the tomb. They said nothing to anyone, because they were afraid. (Mark 16:1-8)

Perhaps if this were the only account of Jesus's resurrection we had read or heard we would not be as surprised as we are, but since we know the stories about Jesus's resurrection from the Gospels of Matthew, Luke, and John we are surprised that the risen Jesus never appears. The women are promised that he will appear, but that is an assurance for the future.

What is even more puzzling is that according to this text the women do not tell anyone what the young man has told them, so we are not sure how Jesus's disciples and Peter are supposed to know about Jesus's future appearance in Galilee.

If we were hearing or reading this text in Greek we might be even more surprised because the text seems to end in the middle of a sentence. It is not impossible to compose a Greek sentence like this, but it is almost unheard of. We cannot quite catch the oddness in English, but it is more as if the sentence ends with "because" rather than with "afraid."

No wonder some early believer who copied Mark's Gospel thought that he should finish the apparently unfinished book by adding a vivid narrative based on the other Gospels at hand.

However, if Mark really thinks that the title of his book is "the beginning of the Gospel" we can see why he leaves the end of the Gospel incomplete. The Gospel is not completed with the story of Jesus, even including the empty tomb. The Gospel is continued in the words and deeds of those who read and hear this story.

Put in other words, when Mark thinks about who Jesus was he also thinks about who Jesus is, and the way to understand Mark's Christology is not just to remember Jesus but to follow him. It is not just to hear the Gospel but to proclaim the Gospel. Understanding Christology in the terms of Mark's book requires following Jesus as well.

What Is that Secret? And Why?

There are a number of places in Mark's Gospel where Jesus tells the disciples to be quiet and tell no about who he is and what he has done; for instance in Mark 8:30 after Peter tells Jesus that Jesus is the Messiah, Jesus "ordered them not to tell anyone about him." And in Mark 9, after a group of the disciples have seen Jesus transfigured into a glorious figure talking with Moses and Elijah, "he ordered them not to tell anyone what they had seen until after the Human One had risen from the dead" (Mark 9:9).

There seem to be several reasons why Mark regularly insists that the disciples stay quiet about who he is.

First, the fullness of who Jesus is can be known only after his resurrection. As the centurion will recognize what it means to say that Jesus is the Son of God only in the light of the cross, the disciples will come to recognize what it means to say that Jesus is the Son of God only in the light of the empty tomb, and perhaps in the light of those appearances that are predicted to happen in Galilee after the time of the narrative has ended (see Mark 16:7).

Second, the full understanding of who Jesus is comes not at the beginning of discipleship but only as the disciples continue to follow Jesus in the way. Before they can really know who he is, the disciples have to obey him.

The fact that the disciples so regularly misunderstand Jesus in Mark's Gospel is not a way of criticizing the disciples' role in the story. Nor is it a way for Mark to condemn those disciples like Peter who have continued for many years in the leadership of the church. It is a way of saying that the road to understanding leads through the hard life of following and sacrifice: those who lose their lives will find them. Those who give up everything to follow Jesus will find him as the Son of God and Messiah that he really is.

The Coming Son of Man

One of the striking features of Mark's narrative is that Jesus often speaks of himself in the third person, and when he does so he regularly designates himself as "the Son of Man." It seems likely that Jesus's use of this phrase for himself comes from the interpretation of Daniel 7, a prophecy of the end of time, which says, in the more narrow translation:

As I watched in the night visions,

> *I saw one like a Son of Man,*
> *coming with the clouds of heaven.*
> *And he came to the Ancient of Days*
> *and was presented before him.*
> *To him was given dominion*
> *and glory and kingship,*
> *that all peoples, nations, and languages*
> *should serve him.*
> *His dominion is an everlasting dominion*
> *that shall not pass away,*
> *And his kingship is one.* (Dan 7:13-14 NRSV)

When Jesus speaks of the end of the age in Mark 13 he echoes the prophecy from Daniel:

But in those days, after that suffering,

> *The sun will be darkened*
> *And the moon will not give its light,*
> *And the stars will be falling from heaven,*
> *And the powers in the heavens will be shaken,*

Then they will see "the Son of Man coming in clouds" with great power and glory. Then he will send out his angels and gather the elect from the four winds, from the ends of the earth to the ends of heaven. (Mark 13:24-27 NRSV)

By this time in Mark's Gospel it is quite clear that when Jesus refers to the Son of Man he refers to himself and that Jesus identifies himself as the one who will appear at the end of time to establish fully the kingdom of God.

That same prediction that Jesus makes to his disciples he makes to the high priest at his trial:

The high priest asked him, "Are you the Messiah [or the Christ], the Son of the Blessed one?"[8] Jesus said, "I am; and

> *'you will see the Son of Man*
> *seated at the right hand of the Power,'*
> *and 'coming with the clouds of heaven.'"* (Mark 14:61-62 NRSV).

"The Power" is surely a name for God, the Ancient of Days in Daniel's picture, but just as surely God's power is contrasted to the passing power of the High Priest. It is in part because Jesus claims to represent that greater power, that contentious power, that the high priest says, "You've heard his insult against God" (Mark 14:64). As in Mark 13, the Son of Man is the representative of the Ancient of Days, his regent on earth.

We saw in chapter 2 that Jesus uses the designation of himself as "Son of Man" also in contexts in which he invokes his authority to forgive sins and in contexts in which he predicts his own suffering, death, and resurrection.

Matthew and Luke also pick up from Mark this use of *Son of Man* as a self-designation for Jesus with a variety of implications. However, it seems likely that Mark is the first writer consistently to equate the prediction in Daniel about the coming Son of Man with Jesus's prediction of the end of the age. Mark constantly reminds us that the story of Jesus and the claims about his significance are not confined to his earthly life or to the time of our own recorded history. He transcends history as well as inhabits it.

Matthew: The Gospel as a Book of Instructions (Torah)

Matthew writes his Gospel using Mark's basic outline of Jesus's story and including most of Mark's material in his own newer Gospel. He also includes a great deal of material—mostly teachings—that he has in common with the Gospel of Luke and tells some stories that are his alone.

Matthew has edited the material he borrowed and the material he added into five great sermons, each one preceded and followed by a section of narrative.

Benjamin Bacon, the Yale scholar of the first part of the twentieth century, thinks that Matthew deliberately sets up his Gospel as a new Torah, or an imitation and supplement to the first five books of the Hebrew Bible.[9]

When Christians translate the Hebrew word *Torah* we usually translate it as "law," but Jewish scholars remind us that the Torah is not just law—as in a rule book—the Torah is a book of instructions and examples.

Unfortunately, because of the fall of Jerusalem in 70 CE, we do not have much Jewish literature from Matthew's time. However the writings of the rabbis a few centuries later often include references to rabbis who would have lived in the first century, and there was undoubtedly some continuity between first-century rabbis and their later disciples.

In any case, for the later rabbis their commentary on scripture (collected in the Talmud) included two main sections. One section was *haggadah*, or narrative, which was a series of brief stories that served to illumine and interpret the biblical text the rabbi was studying. The other section was *halakah*, literally "walking," in which the rabbis suggested to faithful readers how they should walk and behave according to the particular scripture.

Matthew's Gospel looks like an interweaving of *haggadah* and *halakah*. The five sermons in Matthew 5–7, 10, 13, 18, and 23–25 are preceded and followed by stories that help ground them in Jesus's ministry and suggest their implications for those who follow him.

In this book of directions for Christians are several key themes.

Fulfillment

Perhaps most important for Matthew, Jesus is the fulfillment of the Hebrew Bible or of the Old Testament. He is the fulfillment first because the Old Testament or the Hebrew Bible points to him.

For Matthew, the Old Testament time and again testifies to Jesus's identity and validates his mission. A simple example can represent this claim found throughout Matthew's Gospel. When Jesus is born, King Herod plots to destroy him. Joseph, Jesus's adoptive father, is warned in a dream to take him to Egypt where Joseph, Mary, and Jesus remain until after Herod's death. Matthew informs us: "This fulfilled what the Lord had spoken through the prophet: I have called my son out of Egypt'" (Matt 2:15).[10]

Further, we have seen that Matthew shows how Joseph in the New Testament is foreshadowed and predicted by the stories of Joseph in the Old Testament—another dreamer, another visitor to Egypt. This foreshadowing is called typology, and just as the first Joseph is a type of the second, Moses is a type of Jesus. In Jesus Matthew sees a new Moses, a new lawgiver for God's people.

This is evident in the way Matthew tells the story of Jesus's first great sermon, the Sermon on the Mount. Here is how the account begins: "Now when Jesus saw the crowds, he went up a mountain. He sat down and his disciples came to him. He taught them, saying…" (Matt 5:1-2). Almost certainly the first readers or hearers of this account would remember Moses and the giving of the law: "The LORD came down on Mount Sinai to the top of the mountain. The LORD called Moses to come up to the top of the mountain, and Moses went up" (Exod 19:20).

From the Sermon on the Mount to the end of the Gospel we can certainly see how frequently Jesus appears in Matthew's Gospel as teacher and interpreter of the Law, the Torah.

As we have seen, for Jewish people of the first century and to this day, the word *Torah* that we often translate "law" did not just mean a set of rules. In the Sermon on the Mount, Jesus goes on to provide a picture and a guide for living the faithful life. What is clear for Matthew, though, is that Jesus's teaching is to be seen as an interpretation and elaboration of Moses's teaching, not as a replacement. So Jesus says: "Don't even begin to think that I have come to do away with the Law and the Prophets. I haven't come to do away with them but to fulfill them" (Matt 5:17).[11] For Matthew, when Jesus fulfills the Jewish law, he expands and deepens it. He becomes the new Moses not only in who he is but also in what he teaches.

In Matthew when Jesus interprets the Torah he does not merely repeat it. This is most clear in that section of the Sermon on the Mount that scholars call "the antitheses," which is a series of sayings in which Jesus quotes from the Torah and then interprets the teaching for the first-century followers of Jesus. Here is one example:

> You have heard that it was said to those who lived long ago, *Don't commit murder* [or, more traditionally, "you shall not kill"], and all who commit murder will be in danger of judgment.[12] But I say to you that everyone who is angry with [a] brother or sister will be in danger of judgment. If they say to their brother or sister, "You idiot," they will be in danger of being condemned by the governing council. And if they say, "You fool," they will be in danger of fiery hell. (Matt 5:21-22)

The phrase *you have heard that it was said to those who lived long ago* is a polite way of saying what every first-century believer would know it meant: "Moses told you." So when Jesus says, "Moses told you the following, and/but I'm telling you something else," we can see both the continuity and the contrast. Even when Matthew doesn't stop to tell us that Jesus speaks with unique authority (as Matthew does say at the end of the Sermon on the Mount, in Matthew 7:29), Matthew shows us that authority. This teacher is so remarkable that he can elaborate the words of Moses.

In this section of the antitheses it is clear that Jesus is not taking back what Moses said; he is applying it ever more broadly. It is hard to find the right word to describe what Jesus does here. He does not simply "spiritualize" the law, as if it no longer had physical implications. He does not simply "internalize" the law, as if it no longer applied to conduct. He seems rather to suggest that the commandment is everything that Moses said, and even more.

If I am angry enough with another to say, "I wish you were dead," then in the imaginations of my heart I have committed murder; I have treated another person as expendable. That is itself a violation of the commandment.

So with the command to avoid adultery, to practice love of the neighbor, not to swear false oaths, to divorce according to legal requirements, Jesus, as Moses's heir and interpreter, fulfills the Torah by making clear the depth of its implications and the breadth of its applications.

The Last Temptation of Christ

One good way to discover Matthew's understanding of the story of Jesus is to see the changes he makes in the basic outline and even the wording that he takes over from the Gospel of Mark.

For both Mark and Matthew, Jesus's public activity begins with his baptism by John the Baptist followed immediately by the story of Jesus being tempted, or tested, in the wilderness by Satan. In Mark's Gospel this account is very brief and takes up only two verses: "At once the Spirit forced Jesus out into the wilderness. He was in the wilderness for forty days, tempted by Satan. He was among the wild animals, and the angels took care of him" (Mark 1:12-13).

At this point in the story both Matthew and Luke provide a much fuller account of Jesus's temptation by Satan; probably their version of the story depends on that written source that they both had but that we no longer have that scholars call "Q."

For Matthew's Gospel the temptation story—Matthew 4:1-11—provides a kind of overture to the whole of Jesus's ministry. In the overture to an opera or to a musical comedy, the composer often includes musical themes and phrases that will be developed more fully in the rest of the show. The audience begins to anticipate what is coming, and when the star bursts into full song, the audience may think, "I kind of remember that."

Here is Matthew's much more elaborate version of the brief account in Mark:

> Then the Spirit led Jesus up into the wilderness so that the devil might tempt him. After Jesus had fasted for forty days and forty nights, he was starving. The tempter came to him and said, "Since you are God's Son, command these stones to become bread."
>
> Jesus replied, "It's written, *People won't live only by bread, but by every word spoken by God.*"
>
> After that the devil brought him into the holy city and stood him at the highest point of the temple. He said to him, "Since you are God's Son, throw yourself down; for it is written, *I will command my angels concerning you, and they will take you up in their hands so that you won't hit your foot on a stone.*"
>
> Jesus replied, "Again, it's written, *Don't test the Lord your God.*"
>
> Then the devil brought him to a very high mountain and showed him all the kingdoms of the world and their glory. He said, "I'll give you all these if you bow down and worship me."
>
> Jesus responded, "Go away, Satan, because it's written, *You will worship the Lord your God and serve only him.*" The devil left him, and angels came and took care of him. (Matt 4:1-11)

When we compare these verses with Mark's brief story of Jesus's temptation, we notice both the places where Matthew takes over Mark's story and the ways in which he (and his source) elaborate on that story.

In both stories it is the Spirit that drives Jesus into the wilderness. The Spirit has been the sign of God's adoption of Jesus in Mark, of God's acclamation of Jesus in Matthew. In both Gospels the same Spirit that represents God's favor represents God's sovereignty when by the Spirit God drives his Son into the wilderness for temptation.

In both stories Jesus is in the wilderness for forty days and forty nights, surely a recollection of the testing of the children of Israel for forty years in the wilderness in the Hebrew Bible.

In both stories angels minister to Jesus at the end, which is a sign that he has passed the test; it is proof of God's favor (Mark1:13; Matt 4:11).

In Mark we are given no dialogue between Jesus and the tempter. There is only the brief note that "he was among the wild animals" (Mark 1:13). Perhaps the wild animals represent the forces that test and oppose the Son of God. Perhaps they represent Isaiah's picture of the final reign of God when:

> *The wolf will live with the lamb,*
>   *and the leopard will lie down with the young goat;*
>   *the calf and the young lion will feed together,*
>   *and a little child will lead them. (Isa 11:6)*

The extensive dialogue of Matthew 4:1-11 represents a kind of scriptural battle between Jesus and the tempter. Jesus three times finds the verse to counter and trump Satan's verse. Overwhelmingly the scriptural quotations are from the book of Deuteronomy, which is set during Israel's sojourn in the wilderness. The scriptural quotations therefore underline the close connection between Israel's test in the wilderness and Jesus's own.

One of the gifts of biblical study in the last few decades is that scholars have helped us think about a biblical writing, not just as it was originally read or heard, but as it has influenced preachers, theologians, poets, novelists, painters, and composers ever since.[13]

The temptation story in Matthew provides the background for one of the most powerful parables in European literature. In Fyodor Dostoevsky's novel *The Brothers Karamazov* one of the brothers, Ivan, tells his brother, Alyosha, the story of the Grand Inquisitor.[14]

The Grand Inquisitor is assigned the task of trying to strengthen and enforce the power of the Catholic Church. One night he is visited by Jesus. The inquisitor tells Jesus that he missed his chance to do genuine good for humankind by leaving people too much freedom. The inquisitor reminds Jesus of Satan's three temptations, as we find them in Matthew's Gospel.

The first temptation—the temptation of turning the stones into bread—is the temptation of miracle. The second temptation—the suggestion that Jesus throw himself from the temple—is the temptation of mystery. The third temptation—that Jesus become ruler over the world and its empires—is the temptation of authority.

Jesus would have been a much more effective Messiah, the inquisitor suggests, had he chosen miracle, mystery, and authority rather than leaving people the difficult freedom to choose for him or against him.

Dostoevsky's story was written as part of a rich, complicated study of one family and nineteenth-century Russian society, of the contrast between the Catholic Church and the Orthodox church and the contrast between any institutional church and Jesus himself.

What Dostoevsky catches powerfully in our story is the claim that for Matthew, Jesus will not trick people into believing or force them into faith. Jesus's story is the story of one who chooses humility and service even to the point of the cross. Matthew's invitation is for his readers to serve Jesus by following the same path.

So when we come toward the end of Jesus's story in Matthew, when we come to the crucifixion, we see that Matthew takes Mark's story of Jesus's death and adds his own detail. As in Mark's Gospel bystanders mock Jesus as he draws toward his death, but here only the words of the bystanders echo precisely the earlier words of Satan.

Satan has said, "If you are the Son of God, throw yourself down" (Matt 4:6 NRSV). Now the bystanders say: "You who would destroy the temple and build it in three days.... If you are the Son of God, come down from the cross" (Matt 27:40 NRSV).

But for Matthew it is precisely because he *is* the Son of God that Jesus cannot come down from the cross. He would become an entirely different kind of Messiah were he to save himself. Rather his ministry from first to last is to save others. The taunting invitation to come down from the cross does in fact prove the last temptation of Christ.[15]

Making Disciples

For Matthew Jesus is like Moses because he is a great teacher of God's Torah—God's instruction. He is greater than Moses, but that is because he is the greater teacher, the truer interpreter. For Matthew, Jesus is also like the rabbis of Matthew's own time. The Gospel of Matthew was almost certainly written by a Christian who had grown in the synagogue, and it was written for other Christians who had been or even still were synagogue members as the church broadened its mission to the world. It is a Gospel written by a Jewish Christian for Jewish Christians as they move toward a community that includes Gentiles too.

In Matthew's time and in the centuries that follow there was a tradition that a rabbi would gather around himself disciples. In Greek the word *disciple* comes from the verb "to learn as a pupil," and a disciple is one who has been instructed by a teacher. In English we make the link between the person who is a *disciple* and what he or she learns, which is a *discipline* (like the discipline of mathematics or philosophy). But in the New Testament especially it is also the case that a disciple is one who is *disciplined* by the teacher. A disciple is not only a learner; a disciple is a follower.

All the Gospel writers use the term *disciples* for a select group of those who accompany Jesus on his ministry. In all four Gospels the term *disciples* is sometimes used to refer to the twelve, and sometimes the term is used somewhat more broadly.

It is above all Matthew who stresses discipleship as the heart of faithfulness for those who were with Jesus during his life and death, for those who continue to follow after the resurrection, and for those who will be part of the Christian community in the decades and perhaps even the centuries to follow.

Matthew includes five great speeches by Jesus, five sets of instruction. The instruction that starts in chapter 5, the Sermon on the Mount, is addressed to the disciples in the presence of the crowds. The instruction of chapter 10 on mission is addressed to the disciples. In chapter 13, the discourse of parables, Jesus begins by addressing a larger audience, but it is clear that there is an inner circle called and chosen to understand Jesus's teaching, and the term Matthew uses for these people is *disciple:*

> That day Jesus went out of the house and sat down beside the lake. Such large crowds gathered around him that he climbed into a boat and sat down. The whole crowd was standing on the shore. He said many things to them in parables: "A farmer went out to scatter seed."... Jesus' disciples came and said to him, "Why do you use parables when you speak

to the crowds?" Jesus replied, "Because they haven't received the secrets of the kingdom of heaven, but you have." (Matt 13:1-3, 10-11)

When Mark records Jesus's same parable speech, he also distinguishes between those who understand and those who don't, but he calls the inner circle "the people around Jesus, along with the Twelve" (Mark 4:10). It is Matthew who here marks the chosen students with his favorite term for followers: they are "disciples."

Jesus's fourth speech in Matthew, chapter 18, concerning the interactions among disciples is directed to the disciples. His speech in chapter 24, about the destruction of the temple and the final coming of the Son of Man, is prompted by a question from the disciples and is again addressed to them.[16]

In Matthew's Gospel, Jesus performs many functions and is called by many titles, but in the story his recurring function is to be a teacher. The term used time and again for those who are devoted to this teacher, who are open to him, is *disciple*.

It is also clear that for Matthew being a disciple is a matter not only of understanding the teacher but also of following the master. The disciples are to practice what he preaches. For Jesus to be faithful to his mission he must be willing to sacrifice everything; for the disciples to be faithful to his mission they must be willing to make the same sacrifice.

> Then Jesus said to his disciples, "All who want to come after me must say no to themselves, take up their cross, and follow me. All who want to save their lives will lose them. But all who lose their lives because of me will find them. Why would people gain the whole world but lose their lives? What will people give in exchange for their lives?" (Matt 16:24-26)

In Mark's Gospel, this is an instruction for the disciples and the larger group of listeners; in Matthew's Gospel, this is instruction for the disciples only.

In Matthew's Gospel Jesus criticizes the Jewish leaders of his time (and through Jesus Matthew probably criticizes some of the Jewish leaders of his time) as incomplete disciples. They have learned the lessons of the Torah, but they do not practice them: "The legal experts and the Pharisees sit on Moses' seat. Therefore, you must take care to do everything they say. But don't do what they do" (Matt 23:2-3).

The first great discourse to the disciples and to the surrounding crowds ends by stressing the relationship between understanding and obedience, between learning and following:

> Not everybody who says to me, "Lord, Lord," will get into the kingdom of heaven. Only those who do the will of my Father who is in heaven will enter. On the Judgment Day, many people will say to me, "Lord, Lord, didn't we prophesy in your name and expel demons in your name and do lots of miracles in your name?" Then I'll tell them, "I've never known you. Get away from me, you people who do wrong."
>
> Everybody who hears these words of mine and puts them into practice is like a wise builder who built a house on bedrock. The rain fell, the floods came, and the wind blew and beat against that house. It didn't fall because it was firmly set on. But everybody who hears these words of mine and doesn't put them into practice will be like a fool who built a house on the sand. The rain fell, the floods came, and the wind blew and beat against that house. It fell and was completely destroyed. (Matt 7:21-27)

The final words of the risen Lord in Matthew's Gospel, and the final words of the Gospel itself, make clear how essential it is for Matthew that Jesus was the teacher who recruited pupils and followers, and how essential it is that the church continues to teach and to enlist new disciples. And of course it is the disciples who receive the promise and the mandate for discipleship:

> Now the eleven disciples went to Galilee, to the mountain where Jesus told them to go. When they saw him, they worshipped him, but some doubted. Jesus came near and spoke to them, "I've received all authority in heaven and on earth. Therefore, go and make disciples of all nations, baptizing them in the name of the Father and of the Son and of the Holy Spirit, teaching them to obey everything that I've commanded you. Look, I myself will be with you every day until the end of this present age." (Matt 28:16-20)

For Further Reading

Broadhead, Edwin K. *Naming Jesus: Titular Christianity in the Gospel of Mark*. Sheffield: Sheffield Academic, 1999.

Carter, Warren. *Matthew and Empire: Initial Explorations*. Harrisburg: Trinity Press International, 2001.

———. *Telling Tales about Jesus: An Introduction to the New Testament Gospels*. Minneapolis: Fortress, 2016.

Fowler, Robert. *Let the Reader Understand: Reader Response Criticism and the Gospel of Mark*. Philadelphia: Fortress, 1991.

Gregory, Andrew, ed. *The New Proclamation Commentary on the Gospels*. Minneapolis: Fortress, 2006.

Gustafson, James M. *Christ and the Moral Life*. Louisville: Westminster John Knox, 2008.

Henderson, Suzanne Watts. *Christology and Discipleship in the Gospel of Mark*. Cambridge: Cambridge University Press, 2006.

Kazantzakis, Nikos. *The Last Temptation of Christ*. Translated by P. A. Bien. New York: Simon and Schuster, 1960.

Kingsbury, Jack Dean. *Conflict in Mark*. Minneapolis: Augsburg Fortress, 1989.

Luz, Ulrich. *Studies in Matthew*. Grand Rapids: Eerdmans, 2005.

Malbon, Elizabeth Strothers. *Mark's Jesus*. Waco: Baylor, 2009.

Yoder, John Howard. *The Politics of Jesus*. 2nd ed. Grand Rapids: Eerdmans, 1994.

Chapter 9

Stories about Jesus: The Gospels (Luke and John)

Readers of the New Testament have always noticed that John's Gospel is quite different from Mark, Matthew, and Luke. One way of understanding this difference has been to suggest that Mark, Matthew, and Luke all tell the story of Jesus—of course in somewhat different ways—while John gives us a theological reflection on that story.

For many years it has been clear that Mark, Matthew, and Luke are also theological reflections on the story of Jesus. We have come increasingly to appreciate both the artistry and the theological depth that have shaped all four of the Gospels. Matthew, Mark, and Luke of course look more like one another than they do like John, but that is in part because all three of them follow the same outline—that is, Mark's outline. Two of them, Matthew and Luke, almost certainly share another source, the one we call "Q."

Yet though Luke shares Mark's plot and Matthew's literary sources, he has his distinctive way of representing the significance of Jesus. This distinctiveness is especially evident in the fact that Luke's book is really two volumes—the Gospel of Luke and the Acts of the Apostles. It is a significant theological decision to present Jesus's story as climax of the history that precedes him but also as the foundation for the history that follows. The story of Jesus becomes the story of the church, and Luke is the historian of that movement of followers who become the Christian community.

As we shall see, John is also deeply concerned for the ongoing life of his Christian community, but he encompasses his vision for the church in the story of Jesus and the first circle of disciples. The church that Jesus predicts and prays for is the church John hopes will be embodied in his own time.

In this chapter we will look at the somewhat different stories that Luke and John tell and the somewhat different claims they make about the protagonist of that story, Jesus of Nazareth.

Luke: A History

Luke is the only Gospel writer who is explicit about his purpose in writing his Gospel. He begins his Gospel by addressing someone called Theophilus. There are several possible explanations for this name. First, of course, it may have been the name of a specific first-century person, perhaps a patron who helped sponsor Luke's writings. Authors for many centuries have taken the prefaces of their work to thank the person who served as their patron. Or Theophilus may have been a nickname used for a person or for any one of a group of persons who were curious about Jesus. The name when translated into English means "friend of God." It appears from the book of Acts that some early believers in Jesus had been "God-fearers"—Gentiles who knew the Hebrew Bible and accepted much of its doctrine but did not come under the whole discipline of the Torah (see Acts 10:22; 13:16, 26).

Or it may be that the name *Theophilus* can be better translated as "one who loves God" and that Theophilus is a kind of imaginative construct, an ideal reader—rather like the "gentle reader" beloved of certain nineteenth-century authors. In Luke 10:27, Jesus affirms that for those who seek eternal life, it is the obligation of believers to "love the Lord your God with all your heart, with all your being, with all your strength, and with all your mind." Perhaps the Gospel of Luke and the book of Acts, which is its sequel, are dedicated to the kind of Christian or seeker who wishes to love God in just that way.

Stories about Jesus: The Gospels (Luke and John)

Here is the prologue:

> Many people have already applied themselves to the task of compiling an account of the events that have been fulfilled among us. They used what the original eyewitnesses and servants of the word handed down to us. Now, after having investigated everything carefully from the beginning, I have also decided to write a carefully ordered account for you, most honorable Theophilus. I want you to have confidence in the soundness of the instruction you have received. (Luke 1:1-4)

In these verses Luke explicitly identifies himself as a historian. In the first century of the Common Era historians were not supposed simply to recount what happened in the history they are recounting, they were supposed to make sense of that history and often to draw moral or theological or patriotic points.

When Luke says that he wants to "set down an orderly account" based on "eyewitnesses" he sounds very much like a historian of our time whose job is to gather the evidence about a person or an event and to write an account of that evidence in orderly fashion. However, there are clear signs here that Luke also wants his readers to understand the ongoing significance of the story he tells. It is not only witnesses that he turns to for testimony but also "servants of the word." That is, Luke is concerned with the testimony of those who have committed themselves to following Jesus and to preaching and teaching the word about him.

Furthermore when Luke says that he wants Theophilus to "know the truth concerning the things about which you have been instructed" (v. 4), the New Revised Standard Version translation of *truth* misses some of the nuances of the Greek term. Luke wants to provide not only truth for the mind but also certainty, security, assurance—almost spiritual safety—for the believer. Luke wants to draw out the lasting implications of the story he tells. He turns to the testimony of the first believers in order to encourage belief in Theophilus himself, to provide assurance and safety.

Nonetheless, for Luke, the historical context of the Gospel matters. He alone of the four biblical Gospel writers dates Jesus's birth according to the Roman rulers of the time: "In those days Caesar Augustus declared that everyone throughout the empire should be enrolled in the tax lists. This first enrollment occurred when Quirinius governed Syria" (Luke 2:1-2).

Luke's telling of the Gospel makes at least four claims about Jesus that are clearer here than in any of the other Gospels.

The Prophet

First, Luke understands Jesus to be a prophet, in the great traditions of the prophets of Israel and Judah. In our popular language today a prophet is someone who foretells the future, and there is a fair amount of foretelling in the prophetic books in the Hebrew Bible. But what is consistent about the Hebrew prophets is that they claim to speak quite directly and authoritatively for God. They call attention to what God is doing in human history. Sometimes what they see calls for repentance; sometimes what they see calls for hope. In any case, whenever they describe the situation around them or promise a future beyond them, they speak in the conviction that those who hear them should respond.

The fourth chapter of Luke contains an account that is found only in Luke's Gospel. After his testing in the wilderness, Jesus begins his ministry by going to his hometown, Nazareth. He is asked to read scripture for the synagogue and is given the scroll of the prophet Isaiah. He chooses which portion of that prophetic book to read:

> *The Spirit of the Lord is upon me,*
>   *because the Lord has anointed me.*
>
> *He has sent me to preach good news to the poor,*
>   *to proclaim release to the prisoners*
>   *and recovery of sight to the blind,*
>   *to liberate the oppressed,*
>   *and to proclaim the year of the Lord's favor. (Luke 4:18-19)*

Then Jesus rolls up the scroll, hands it back to the attendant, sits down as a synagogue teacher would be expected to do, and says: "Today, this scripture has been fulfilled just as you heard it" (Luke 4:21).

In these verses Jesus chooses as the guide for his ministry words spoken by the prophet Isaiah about the job of the prophet; Isaiah's job description becomes Jesus's job description. But more than that, Luke suggests that Isaiah's words do not apply exclusively to Isaiah. The prophet prophesies about what a prophet should do. Jesus says: "This prophecy was about me; I am the true prophet."

Luke reinforces his picture of Jesus as prophet with what comes next. Jesus stirs up something of a controversy with his own townspeople over whether he is treating them as well as he does the towns around him. Jesus responds by saying: "No prophet is acceptable in his hometown." Then he compares himself to Elijah and Elisha. Both of them were great prophets who were also rejected by their own townspeople. So Jesus identifies himself with Isaiah, Elijah, and Elisha; he, too, is one of the prophets and the true fulfillment of prophecy (Luke 4:24-27).

We notice also that in these verses prophets not only speak for God's reign, but also act out God's reign by the miracles they do. Elijah healed the widow's son at Zarephath; Elisha cured King Naaman. The role of the prophet includes deeds that manifest God's rule. In Luke's Gospel, Jesus the miracle worker is not contrasted to Jesus the teacher; teaching and healing are all part of what it means to be a prophet.

Toward the middle of Luke's Gospel the writer presents a passage that again makes clear how much Jesus's ministry can be seen as that of a prophet. It also reminds the reader of the fate that awaits prophets and that now awaits Jesus, too:

> At that time, some Pharisees approached Jesus and said, "Go! Get away from here, because Herod wants to kill you."
>
> Jesus said to them, "Go, tell that fox, 'Look, I'm throwing out demons and healing people today and tomorrow, and on the third day I will complete my work. However, it's necessary for me to travel today, tomorrow, and the next day because it's impossible for a prophet to be killed outside of Jerusalem.'
>
> "Jerusalem, Jerusalem, you who kill the prophets and stone those who were sent to you! How often I have wanted to gather your people just as a hen gathers her chicks under her wings. But you didn't want that. Look, your house is abandoned. I tell you, you won't see me until

the time comes when you say, *Blessings on the one who comes in the Lord's name."* (Luke 13:31-35)

Now not only are Jesus's mission and rejection part of his prophetic mission; his death in Jerusalem will fulfill that mission as well.

Jesus and the Church

Second, for Luke Jesus is the founder of a community—that is, the church. Luke is the only Gospel writer to write two volumes: the Gospel of Luke and the Acts of the Apostles. When Mark writes his Gospel, the Gospel Luke follows so frequently, he believes that Jesus will return soon to bring about the end of the age and the completion of the kingdom. Those who hear the Gospel need to follow; there is no time or need to organize.

When Luke writes his two books, not only has Jesus finished his earthly ministry, but also the first generation of apostles is passing away. Luke wants to validate the importance of the church and to inspire the church's life by looking to Jesus as the founder of that institution itself.

At the end of Luke's Gospel, in his farewell to his disciples, Jesus instructs them to stay in the city of Jerusalem until they are clothed with power. At the beginning of the book of Acts, the disciples are in the city. They experience a powerful outpouring of the Spirit of God and the church's ministry of spreading the gospel begins (see Acts 2:1-36).

In the way that Luke structures his two volumes we can see the concern for continuity and faithfulness, not just in individual lives, but in the life of a newborn institution—the church.

For Luke, the first authoritative community teacher is Jesus. Jesus guarantees the faithfulness of the ongoing church by appointing a group of apostles to continue his teaching and his activity of doing good. After Jesus's ascension to be with God, the Holy Spirit adds to the company of believers on a regular basis and also adds a late-coming church leader, Paul, to help keep and spread the faith. Finally, toward the end of the two volumes, Paul speaks to a group of elders and entrusts the faith and practice of the church to their hands (see Acts 20:17-35).

So for Luke, Jesus is both the last prophet and the first church leader.

Jesus as Martyr

Third, because Luke writes with the church especially in mind, for him Jesus is the first church martyr. If you compare the story of Jesus's death in Luke's Gospel with the story in Mark's Gospel, which Luke had certainly read, you can see how much Luke shapes his story to present Jesus as a faithful believer who dies for his faith. Later in the book of Acts, the first martyr among the believers is Stephen, and a reading of the story of Stephen's heroic martyrdom in Acts 7 will show how close that story is in detail to the account of Jesus's heroic martyrdom in Luke 23.

In some versions of Luke's Gospel, and in no other Gospel, Jesus acts like a good Christian in forgiving his enemies (as he instructed his followers to do in Luke 6:37): "Jesus said: 'Father, forgive them, for they don't know what they're doing'" (Luke 23:34).

In Mark's Gospel, the last words Jesus speaks before he dies are the same as the quotation from Psalm 22: "My God, my God, why have you left me?" (Mark 15:34). Luke undoubtedly knows this story, but his account of Jesus's last words seems composed to give comfort to Christian martyrs in Luke's own time: "Father, into your hands I entrust my life" (Luke 23:46).

In Mark's Gospel the words of the centurion are the first words of a Gentile believer: "This man was certainly God's Son" (Mark 15:39). For Luke, these words are the verdict of an objective eyewitness: "This man was righteous [or as in the NRSV, "innocent"] (Luke 23:47).

For Luke, the prophet who founds the church also provides the church a great example of being faithful even to death.

Jesus: The Forgiveness of God

Jesus's prayer on the cross, "Father, forgive them, for they don't know what they're doing" (Luke 23:34), suggests one final theme for Luke's Gospel. Through the centuries Christians have said that Jesus came to represent and present God's forgiveness. It is Luke in both the Gospel and the book of Acts who most prominently identifies the heart of Jesus's ministry as the forgiveness of sins.

Toward the beginning of the Gospel, Zechariah sings a song about his soon-to-be-born son, John, who will be John the Baptist. John's mission will be to prepare the way for Jesus who prepares the way for God's reign. God's reign will be marked by the forgiveness of sins: "You, child, will be called a prophet of the Most High, for you will go before the Lord to prepare his way. You will tell his people how to be saved through the forgiveness of their sins" (Luke 1:76-77).

In the story of Jesus's crucifixion we are given another example of forgiveness. This story is found only in Luke's Gospel:

> One of the criminals hanging next to Jesus insulted him: "Aren't you the Christ? Save yourself and us!"
>
> Responding, the other criminal spoke harshly to him, "Don't you fear God, seeing that you've also been sentenced to die? We are rightly condemned, for we are receiving the appropriate sentence for what we did. But this man has done nothing wrong." Then he said, "Jesus, remember me when you come into your kingdom."
>
> Jesus replied, "I assure you that today you will be with me in paradise." (Luke 23:39-43)

At the end of Luke's Gospel Jesus, risen from the dead, sums up his mission and commissions the apostles: "This what is written: the Christ will suffer and rise from the dead on the third day, and a change of heart and life for the forgiveness of sins must be preached in his name to all nations, beginning from Jerusalem" (Luke 24:46-47).

At the center of the Gospel is the parable we know as the parable of the prodigal son. The first great section of that parable, which is the story of the younger brother, is itself the story of the son's repentance and the father's forgiveness. Through the power of forgiveness father and son are reunited.

Finally, in writing the book of Acts, Luke had several opportunities to sum up the meaning of Jesus's life, death, and resurrection. We can take such summaries as clues to Luke's perspective on Jesus's activity. Here the Apostle Peter is speaking and ends his speech this way: "All the prophets testify about [Jesus] that everyone who believes in him receives forgiveness of sins through his name" (Acts 10:43; see similarly Acts 13:38 and 26:18).

For Luke, Jesus preached God's forgiveness and enacted God's forgiveness. After the resurrection, those who believe in the risen Jesus still receive forgiveness through him. And for Luke the historian, it is especially vital to see the role of Jesus in history: he stands in the line of the prophets; he initiates the community that will be the church, the historical manifestation of the coming kingdom; he gives an example of faithful suffering in the midst of opposition from emperors and kings; and he embodies the forgiveness of God.

John: The Trial Story

Though John's complex and metaphorical language is quite different from modern courtroom dramas, some of his dramatic devices remind us of the second half of the old *Law and Order* television series or at least the last few chapters of a novel by John Grisham. There are enough twists and turns to satisfy the most demanding fan: the one who appears to be on trial is really the judge; the execution is more of an escape; the surprise witness does not promise to tell the truth "so help me God"; the surprise witness *is* God.

When we come to read the story of Jesus in the Gospel of John we immediately realize how different John's portrait of Jesus is from that of the other Gospel writers. The three first Gospels are called the Synoptic Gospels because they follow the same basic synopsis, or outline. Because there are three of them and only one non-Synoptic Gospel and because Jesus in the first three Gospels acts and speaks in fairly consistent ways, it is easy to think that Mark, Matthew, and Luke portray the real Jesus and that John portrays a kind of extended reflection on Jesus that says more about the author of the Gospel than about its subject.

The nature of Jesus's sermons is very different in John than in the first three Gospels. In Mark, Matthew, and Luke, Jesus speaks either in fairly brief and pithy sayings or in a long discourse that consists of numbers of such sayings knitted together. In John, Jesus speaks in quite long orations, usually around one theme (like the oration on the bread of life in John 6). Indeed, the whole section from John 14–17 is essentially one long sermon on the unity of God the Father, Jesus his son, and the disciples who represent the ongoing life of the church. In the Synoptic Gospels we usually have relatively short parables; in John, we have rather long allegories—on the vine (in chapter 15), for instance, or the good shepherd (in chapter 10).

Even the details of the plot are different in John. In the first three Gospels, Jesus visits the temple in Jerusalem only once as an adult. In John's Gospel, he visits twice. In the first three Gospels, Jesus prays in Gethsemane to be saved from the crucifixion. John's Gospel does not present any such scene. In the first three Gospels, Jesus is baptized by John the Baptizer; in John's Gospel, John the Baptizer bears witness to Jesus but does not baptize him.

Yet we remember that the first three Gospels seem much alike in part because all three contain much of the material from Mark's Gospel, that almost certainly Matthew and Luke had Mark's Gospel before them, and that at many points they copied Mark nearly word for word.

For centuries scholars who wanted to find the "historical" Jesus tended to rely on the Synoptic Gospels as more reliable than John, in part because there are three of them and in part because it is easier for us to imagine the Jesus that we find portrayed there than it is to imagine the rather different picture of Jesus in John's Gospel.

Some recent scholars have urged us to pay more attention to John's Gospel as a source of reliable historical evidence about Jesus, and that is undoubtedly an enterprise worth pursuing.[1] However, another way of rethinking the difference between John and the Synoptic Gospels is to suggest that John makes explicit what is implicit in all four Gospels: this is not a portrait of Jesus composed of irrefutable historical facts and verifiable direct quotations. All four Gospels are portraits more like the work of impressionists like Manet or van Gogh and less like the work of more "photographic" artists like Michelangelo (though, of course, every Michelangelo statue or painting interprets the figure it portrays as well).

That is why in this book on New Testament Christology we have tried to stress that the source of New Testament Christology is found in the texts of the New Testament—in the stories, the parables, and the hymns—rather than in a Jesus we try to reconstruct from those sources: a "real" or "historical" Jesus.

In studying John's Gospel we suggest two themes that mark John's particular perspective on Jesus.

Incarnation

John provides the only explicit discussion of Jesus as being God in human form. The traditional word for the doctrine of God's presence in Jesus is *incarnation,* or "in-fleshment." We saw earlier how the hymn that begins John's Gospel (John 1:1-14) provides one of the earliest claims that God's son was present with the creator from before time began and in Jesus Christ entered into human history. John's claim relies on his reading of Genesis 1 in which God spoke creation into life. Because God *spoke* creation into life, we know that the world was created by a word. John says that God created the world by *the* Word. *Word* (Greek: *logos*) is the name for that creative power who was with God from the beginning and who has come into human life through Jesus Christ.

> *In the beginning was the Word*
> > *and the Word was with God*
> > *and the Word was God.*
>
> *The Word was with God in the beginning.*
>
> *Everything came into being through the Word,*
> > *and without the Word*
> > *nothing came into being*
>
> . . . .
>
> *The Word became flesh*
> > *and made his home among us.*
>
> *We have seen his glory,*
> > *glory like that of a father's only son,*
> > > *full of grace and truth. (John 1:1-3, 14)*

The whole Gospel of John calls us back to this opening hymn about "the Word" in two ways.

First, one way to describe the long and complicated sermons and sayings of this Gospel is to say that Jesus, the Word incarnate, is made known through words. It is not just that John remembers some of Jesus's longer speeches or thinks that when it comes to speaking, more is better. It is that, for John, the words Jesus speaks continue to have creative power as the Word had power at the beginning of creation. The words Jesus speaks themselves give life.

Toward the end of the long discussion on bread in John 6, Jesus sums up this claim about the power of his words: "The words I have spoken to you are spirit and life" (John 6:63). That is, just as the word in Genesis creates the cosmos, the words that Jesus speaks create new life among those who believe in him.

A few verses later some of the disciples are preparing to leave Jesus, and Peter affirms what John affirms, that is, the right human response to the words of the Word made flesh: "Jesus asked the Twelve, 'Do you also want to leave?' Simon Peter answered, 'Lord, where would we go? You have the words of eternal life. We believe and know that you are God's holy one'" (John 6:67-69).

There is another way in which John's Gospel story enacts, enfleshes the first hymn and its claim that Jesus is the Word who was with God and was God. Time after time in John's Gospel, Jesus answers a question or begins a paragraph using the Greek phrase *ego eimi*. The first word, *ego*, is the pronoun meaning "I." In English the word has entered into our vocabulary when we talk about Sigmund Freud's designation of the ego, the superego, and the id; when we want to insult someone else we can always call him or her an egotist. The second word, *eimi*, is a Greek verb that means "I am." It means both the English pronoun and the English verb in that phrase. In many languages—Greek, French, Spanish—I can indicate whether the verb is about the first person, "me," or the second person, "you," or the third person, "he or she or it," without having to include a pronoun at all. The verb itself really does say it all.

So when Jesus says not just, "I am the bread of life," but "I—I am the bread of life," he places a particular stress on his own identity: "I really am the bread of life" or "I myself am the bread of life."

However, as we read the Gospel of John it becomes clear that Jesus does not simply use this odd phrase to emphasize himself; he uses this odd phrase to identify himself in a particular way.

The Christian who wrote John's Gospel and many of the people who would first have heard it were steeped in the Old Testament, the Hebrew Bible. And one passage that every good Jew or friend of Jews would have known comes in Exodus 3:14, in which Moses asks God to give him God's name and God answers and does not answer all at once, by reciting the puzzling phrase: "I AM WHO I AM" (Exod 3:14).[2] In the Greek translation of the Old Testament/Hebrew Bible that John and his readers would have known, this brief but puzzling sentence begins with the two words Jesus so often quotes: *ego eimi*. As John reads Exodus, anyway, the phrase that Jesus uses so often in referring to himself is a part of the deeply mysterious name of the one true God. One reason Jesus uses this phrase so often in John's Gospel is to act out John's claim in the prologue, that the Word was (and is) God and that the Word was (and is) with God.

We can guess that this is the case in many of the places where Jesus uses the phrase *ego eimi*, but we can see it quite clearly in a passage that does not seem filled with theological reflection, when Jesus's opponents come to arrest Jesus in the garden:

> Jesus knew everything that was to happen to him, so he went out and asked, "Who are you looking for?" They answered, "Jesus the Nazarene." He said to them, "I Am." (Judas, his betrayer, was standing with them.) When he said, "I Am," they shrank back and fell to the ground. (John 18:4-6)

They fall to the ground when he claims for himself the divine name; for a moment at least they recognize the presence of God's own self standing before them.

Witness: Testimony

There is a second theme enacted in John's telling of Jesus's story. Looking through John's Gospel we notice how often Jesus uses the term *witness* or *testimony* or *testify*. All these come from the same Greek word, *martyreo*, "I testify" or "I witness." From this same root we take our English word *martyr*—one who brings testimony, bears witness, even at the cost of the martyr's life.

We have suggested that one way to read John's Gospel is as trial story, which is the kind of story that has made novelists like John Grisham both famous and rich. Jesus says at one point that his ministry is essentially to set up court for God on earth:

> God didn't send his Son into the world to judge the world, but that the world might be saved through him. Whoever believes in him isn't judged; whoever doesn't believe in him is already judged, because they don't believe in the name of God's only Son.
> This is the basis for judgment: The light came into the world, and people loved darkness more than the light, for their actions are evil. All who do wicked things hate the light and don't come to the light for fear that their actions will be exposed to the light. Whoever does the truth comes to light so that it can be seen that their actions were done in God. (John 3:17-21)

One way to read John's Gospel is to read it like the last chapters of a Grisham novel or the last fifteen minutes of a *Law and Order* episode. One after another John calls to the stand the "witnesses" who will bear "testimony" to who Jesus really is. Finally those who hear this story or who read this story are the jury. But there is also a twist, as we see in this passage from John 3 and we shall see again in this Gospel. Those of us who are the jury are in fact the ones who are really judged. At the end of the story our verdict on Jesus becomes a verdict on ourselves.

The first witness is John the Baptist.

This is John's testimony when the Jews in Jerusalem sent priests and Levites to ask him: "'Who are you?' John confessed (he didn't deny but confessed), 'I'm not the Christ.... *I am a voice crying out in the wilderness, Make the Lord's path straight*'" (John 1:19-20, 23).

A short while later, when Jesus comes to meet John the Baptist, John takes up his role as witness once again: "I have seen and testified that this one is God's Son" (John 1:34).

The Father who sent Jesus also testifies on his behalf. In John 5:31, Jesus says this: "If I testify about myself, my testimony isn't true." Then

Jesus lists three valid witnesses. John is a valid witness. The works that Jesus has done are witnesses to him: "And the Father who sent me testifies about me. You have never even heard his voice or seen his form, and you don't have his word dwelling with you" (John 5:37-38).

On another other occasion, however, Jesus does become a witness to himself and to his own special status as the one sent from God. He is speaking to his opponents among the synagogue leaders: "In your Law it is written that the witness of two people is true. I am one witness concerning myself, and the Father who sent me is the other" (John 8:17-18; see also the verses just preceding these).

In John's Gospel, after Jesus's death and resurrection, Jesus returns to the Father and completes his journey. In the time after Jesus's departure, the Father sends a kind of substitute; the Greek word is *paraclete*, and the Paraclete, who is the Spirit and presence of God, bears witness to Jesus, too. In the ongoing life of the church, it is the Paraclete who becomes witness for Jesus in the ongoing trial of the world: "When the [Paraclete] comes, whom I will send from the Father—the Spirit of Truth who proceeds from the Father—he will testify about me" (John 15:26).

Inspired by the Paraclete, the disciples will also continue to bear witness: "You will testify too, because you have been with me from the beginning" (15:27). One of those disciples is the beloved disciple, whose testimony has become the basis for the Gospel's depiction of Jesus's crucifixion and on a broader level probably for the whole Gospel itself. After the Gospel writer has described the soldiers piercing Jesus's side with a spear he cites the witness whose testimony has been basic to his story: "The one who saw this has testified, and this testimony is true. He knows that he speaks the truth, and he has testified so that you also can believe" (John 19:35).[3]

Finally, the written Gospel itself becomes a witness to Jesus in the great judgment that separates believers from unbelievers. These are the last words of what is probably the original form of the Gospel: "Then Jesus did many other miraculous signs in his disciples' presence, signs that aren't recorded in this scroll. But these things are written so that you will believe that Jesus is the Christ, God's Son, and that believing, you will have life in his name" (John 20:30-31). Those who believe receive the verdict of rich and abiding life; those who do not believe are sentenced to live deadly lives, whether they know it or not.

Conclusion: The Four Gospels and the Christ They Present

We said at the beginning of this volume that we can better understand the Christology of the New Testament by looking at the kinds of stories Christians tell and the kinds of hymns Christians sing than by looking at explicit statements about doctrine.

The four Gospels use four different kinds of narrative to help us see how Jesus is the Messiah, the Son of God, for each of the Gospel writers. The Gospel writers do not explicitly describe their works in these categories, but the categories can help us understand what the Gospels are doing.

Mark is a drama, and Jesus is the hero. If we had only chapters 1 to 15 we might think that the drama was a tragedy, with the hero dying abandoned and alone and yet in his death inspiring others. Chapter 16 and some of the predictions and prophecies earlier in the Gospel remind us that for Mark, Jesus's story does not end with his death, though how this ending turns tragedy into comedy is not always as clear as early Christians would have hoped.

Matthew is a book of teaching, and Jesus is the great instructor. Like any fine teacher, he lives out his own teachings, but he continues to live in the church as an instructor and an encouragement.

Luke is explicitly a book of history. He sets Jesus as an (the) essential figure in the history of the church and even the history of the world. His protagonist also sets an example for those who seek to follow him, even when that following means danger.

John writes a suspense story like a good trial novel. On one level, it looks as though Jesus is on trial, but by the end of the story we realize that his opponents are on trial and then finally that we the readers are on trial too. The question is whether the readers believe his testimony or not. If they do, it is not that he is vindicated; they are.

There is no doubt that the four writers are writing about the same protagonist. But because they see him somewhat differently and describe him in somewhat different settings, we are left with four different stories in which he is always the essential character, but essential in somewhat different ways.

For Further Reading

Anderson, Paul et al., eds. *John, Jesus and History.* Leiden and Boston: Brill, 2007.

Ashton, John. *The Gospel of John and Christian Origins.* Minneapolis: Fortress, 2014.

Buckwalter, H. Douglas. *The Character and Purpose of Luke's Christology.* SNTMS 89. Cambridge: Cambridge University Press, 1996.

Culpepper, R. Alan. *The Anatomy of the Fourth Gospel.* Philadelphia: Fortress, 1983.

Loader, William. *Christology in the Fourth Gospel.* Frankfurt and New York: P. Lang, 1989 (a new edition is forthcoming).

Ringe, Sharon. *Luke.* Louisville: Westminster John Knox, 1995.

Rowe, C. Kavin. *Early Narrative Christology: The Lord in the Gospel of Luke.* Grand Rapids: Baker Academic, 2006.

Smith, D. Moody. *The Theology of the Gospel of John.* Cambridge and New York: Cambridge University Press, 1999.

Strauss, M. L. *The Davidic Messiah in Luke-Acts: The Promise and Its Fulfillment in Lukan Christology.* Sheffield: Sheffield Academic Press, 1995.

Notes

1. Jesus of Nazareth

1. This is the English translation of the title of the book by Albert Schweitzer—a study and criticism of our attempt to find the "real" Jesus; see *The Quest of the Historical Jesus*, ed. John Bowden, trans. W. Montgomery, J. R. Coates, Susan Cupitt, and John Bowden (1906; Minneapolis, MN: Fortress, 2001).

2. Ibid.

3. Laurie Beth Jones, *Jesus, CEO: Using Ancient Wisdom for Visionary Leadership* (New York: Hyperion, 1995).

4. Norman Perrin, *Rediscovering the Teaching of Jesus* (New York: Harper and Row, 1978).

5. See Robert Funk et al., *The Five Gospels: What Did Jesus Really Say? The Search for the Authentic Words of Jesus* (New York: Macmillan, 1993).

6. E. P. Sanders, *The Historical Figure of Jesus* (London: Penguin, 1993); Dale C. Allison Jr. *Constructing Jesus* (Grand Rapids: Baker Academic, 2010).

7. See Flavius Josephus, *Antiquities*: 18.5.2

8. For New Testament evidence, see Mark 3:19-27; for Jewish evidence from the early centuries of the Common Era, see Peter Schafer, *Jesus in the Talmud* (Princeton, NJ: Princeton University Press, 2007).

2. Jesus's Resurrection: The Turning Point

1. N. T. Wright argues for the probability of Jesus's resurrection on historical grounds (*The Resurrection of the Son of God* [Minneapolis: Fortress, 2003]). Richard Swinburne argues on philosophical grounds (*The Resurrection of God Incarnate* [Oxford: Clarendon, 2003]). Two careful studies suggest different approaches: Hans

Frei, *The Identity of Jesus Christ* (Philadelphia: Fortress, 1975); and Richard R. Niebuhr, *Resurrection and Historical Reason* (New York: Scribner's, 1957).

2. We are not sure, however, what particular scriptural passages Paul may have had in mind.

3. This is where the earliest Greek manuscripts of Mark's Gospel end. Some of our translations include the verses from later manuscripts.

4. John 21 is probably a later addition to the Gospel, but it also reflects the importance of Peter at the resurrection and his somewhat complicated relationship to the Beloved Disciple.

3. Titles for Jesus

1. For a very helpful survey of the use of the term *Christ/Messiah* and indeed on the context of many christological titles, see Adela Yarbro Collins and John J. Collins, *King and Messiah as Son of God* (Grand Rapids: Eerdmans, 2008).

2. Along with many other students of John's Gospel I think that chapter 21 was added sometime after the completion of the original Gospel.

3. We shall discuss the use of hymns in the New Testament in chapter 5.

4. Warren Carter, *Matthew and Empire: Initial Explorations* (Harrisburg: Trinity Press International, 2001), 73. I have omitted scriptural quotations included in the original.

5. See Michael Peppard, *Son of God in the Ancient World: Divine Sonship in Its Social and Political Context* (New York: Oxford University Press, 2001).

6. Early manuscripts have different forms of the verb *to believe*. The first version suggests keeping faithful; the second suggests becoming faithful.

7. Using the translation in the notes of the NRSV. The more generic plural muddles the connection here between humankind and the specific human Jesus. Hebrews itself is quoting Psalm 8:4 in the Greek Old Testament.

4. The Beginning of the Gospel(s)

1. This is the interpretation I prefer. See David L. Bartlett, *What's Good about This News?* (Louisville: Westminster John Knox, 2003), 29–32.

2. Mark tells us that the quotation in Mark 1:2-3 is from the prophet Isaiah; in fact, it is a combination of Isaiah 40:3 and Malachi 3:1.

3. In Malachi 3:23-24 (MT) (4:5-6 LXX), the messenger of 3:1 is identified with Elijah, who will be sent by God for the purpose of reconciliation. Adela Y. Collins, *Mark (Hermeneia)* (Minneapolis: Fortress, 2007), 136.

4. In some early manuscripts of Luke's Gospel it is Elizabeth and not Mary who sings this song.

5. Allen Verhey, *The Great Reversal* (Grand Rapids: Eerdmans, 1984).

6. For a helpful discussion of wisdom and John's Gospel, see Sharon Ringe, *Wisdom's Friends: Community and Christology in the Fourth Gospel* (Louisville: Westminster John Knox, 1999).

7. For similar understandings of *wisdom*, see Sirach 24:3 and Wisdom 9:1-2 in the Apocrypha. For a discussion of the relationship of this literature to John's Gospel, see Raymond E. Brown, *The Gospel According to John*, vol. 1 of The Anchor Bible Series (Garden City: Doubleday, 1966), 521–24.

5. Singing about Jesus: Hymns and Prayers in the New Testament

1. Walt Whitman, "When Lilacs Last in the Dooryard Bloom'd," Poetry Foundation, https://www.poetryfoundation.org/poems-and-poets/poems/detail/45480. Public domain.

2. Jack T. Sanders, *The New Testament Christological Hymns: Their Historical Religious Background* (Cambridge: Cambridge University Press, 1971), 9–25.

3. See Henry H. Mitchell, *Celebration and Experience in Preaching* (Nashville: Abingdon Press, 1990).

4. The hymns we discuss correspond in most cases to the hymns noted in Jack T. Sanders, *The New Testament Christological Hymns*.

5. These two lines include a quotation from Isaiah 45:23.

6. The division of the stanzas is Sanders's adaptation of Lohmeyer (Sanders, *New Testament Christological Hymns*, 9). The translation is my own.

7. This is a variation of the interpretation by James Dunn in *Christology in the Making*, 2nd ed. (Grand Rapids: Eerdmans, 1981), 114–21.

8. There is an excellent discussion of these issues in Raymond E. Brown, *John*, 20–21.

9. The NRSV makes this the last line of the verse, transposing the last two lines of the Greek.

6. Practical Christology: Paul and His Letters

1. There are many who think that 2 Corinthians is really composed of several letters brought together by a later editor. But whether 2 Corinthians 4 and

2 Corinthians 8 were originally part of the same letter, they were both words written by Paul to the congregation at Corinth.

2. For a fuller discussion of the situation of the Roman churches, see Leander Keck, *Romans* (Nashville: Abingdon Press, 2005), and David Bartlett, *Romans* (Louisville: Westminster John Knox, 1995).

3. This is a mix of my own translation and the CEB.

4. For a fuller discussion of Paul's understanding of sin and justification, see Bartlett, *Romans*, 30–35, 60–71.

5. I suspect that the letter to the Ephesians was written by one of Paul's followers, in his name. It was probably written shortly after Paul's death. For that letter there are not only "churches" but also "the church"—the community that includes the other communities and can be the perfect bride of Christ.

7. Stories Jesus Tells

1. C. H. Dodd, *Parables of the Kingdom* (New York: Scribner's, 1961).

2. For a very helpful contemporary discussion of "grace," see Marilynne Robinson, "Grace," in *The Givenness of Things* (New York: Farrar, Strauss and Giroux, 2015), 31–49.

3. See William Herzog, *Parables as Subversive Speech* (Louisville: Westminster John Knox, 1996), 79–96.

4. For a splendid discussion of the "original" intent of the story and its subsequent interpretations, see Ulrich Luz, *Matthew*, trans. W. C. Linns (Philadelphia: Fortress, 2005), 3:266–84.

5. The phrase might also be *all the Gentiles*; see Luz, *Matthew*, for discussion. With either translation the sovereignty of Jesus over history is clear.

8. Stories about Jesus: The Gospels (Mark and Matthew)

1. See Jack Dean Kingsbury, *Conflict in Mark* (Minneapolis: Augsburg Fortress, 1989).

2. Shakespeare, *Hamlet*, act 5, scene 2.

3. Taken from a personal conversation.

4. Shakespeare, *Cymbeline*, act 5, scene 5.

5. Shakespeare, *The Winter's Tale*, act 5, scene 3.

6. William Wrede, *The Messianic Secret*, trans. J. C. G. Greig (Cambridge: J Clarke, 1971).

7. In the Greek text it is possible that the centurion says, "Truly this was *a* son of God," but the whole dramatic structure of the Gospel makes this unlikely.

8. Notice that these are in effect the two titles Mark gives to Jesus in Mark 1:1.

9. Benjamin Wisner Bacon, *Studies in Matthew* (New York: Henry Holt, 1930).

10. The quotation is from Jeremiah 31:15.

11. Probably in Matthew's time there were some Christians who thought that they were freed from obligation to the Law of Moses or that as Gentiles they did not need to pay much attention to it. Some readings of the Apostle Paul's writings could easily lead in that direction.

12. Or "but I say to you." The Greek word could mean either, but that does not imply the absolute contrast that Matthew would imply by using another word for *but*.

13. This is known as *history of effects* or *reception history*. Ulrich Luz is a student of Matthew's Gospel who uses this method very helpfully. See, for instance, his discussion of Matthew 4 in *Matthew*, vol. 1, trans. J. E. Crouch (Philadelphia: Fortress, 2007), 153–56.

14. Fyodor Dostoevsky, *The Brothers Karamazov*, trans. Richard Pevear and Larissa Vokokhosnsky (New York: Farrar Strauss and Giroux, 1990), 256–64.

15. This is another example of the history of effects. See Nikos Kazantzakis, *The Last Temptation of Christ*, trans. P. A. Bien (New York: Simon and Schuster, 1960).

16. In Mark 13, the disciples raise the same question, about the temple, but the discourse is directed to a smaller inner circle.

9. Stories about Jesus: The Gospels (Luke and John)

1. See, for instance, Paul N. Anderson et al., eds., *John, Jesus and History* (Leiden and Boston: Brill, 2007).

2. I rely on the NRSV translation here, but the saying really is puzzling in the Hebrew and not much less so in the Greek translation of the book of Exodus.

3. Many scholars think that John 21 was written somewhat later than the rest of John's Gospel, but in any case John 21:24 makes a similar claim about the beloved disciple: "This is the disciple who testifies concerning these things and who wrote them down. We know that his testimony is true." I think that this refers to the beloved disciple as a source for the Gospel but not as its author.

Scripture Index

Old Testament

Genesis
1. 153
1:1 . . . . 39, 46, 65, 67
1:3 . . . . 14, 54
2–3 . . . . 89, 91
12:1-3 45
22 32

Exodus
3:14 . . . . 29, 155
19:20 133

1 Samuel
16 24
16:12-13 25

Psalms
2:7 . . . . 30, 44, 126
22 . . . . 127, 149
23 99
110:1 28

Proverbs
3:19 . . . . 55, 56
8:22-23 55
29–31 55

Isaiah
7 51
7:14 . . . . 46, 47
11:6 137

Daniel
7:13 . . . . 33, 34
7:13-14 130

New Testament

Matthew
1:2 49
1:17 46
1:21 46
1:23 . . . . 1, 46, 47
1:25 . . . . 46, 51
2:1-12 . . . . 48, 50
2:2 48
2:15 133
4:1-11 136–38
4:11 136
4:17 101
5:1-2 133
5:21-22 134
6 10
7:21-27 141
7:29 134
8:20 81
13 99
13:1-3, 10-11 140
13:24 101
13:45-46 99
16:15-17 26
18 140
18:20 47
20 99
20:1-16 . . . . . . 100, 107, 111–12, 119

24. 140	14:61-62 . . . . 35, 131
25 102	14:64 131
25:1 116	15:10-14 97
25:14 116	15:21 122
25:31-46 115	15:34 . . . . 127, 149
25:32 117	15:39 . . . . 32, 123, 126, 149
27:40 138	15:40-41 122
28. 18	16:1-8 . . . . 17, 128
28:16-20 141	16:6 125
28:19 5	16:7 129
28:20 47	16:9-20 127

Mark

Luke

1:1 . . . . . 1, 25, 31, 40, 41, 46, 126, 127	1. 50
1:1-3 53	1:1-4 144
1:2-4 41	1:31 51
1:7-8 43	1:37 50
1:9-11 30	1:76-77 150
1:11 . . . . 31, 42, 122, 126	2:1-20 50
1:12-13 135	2:14 . . . . 49, 52
1:13 136	3. 39
1:14-15 43	3:23 49
2:1-12 35	3:23-38 49
3:11 126	4:18-19 146
4. 98	4:21 146
4:1-9 100	4:24-27 147
4:11 . . . . 13, 30, 99	6:37 149
4:13-20 100	7. 14
4:26-27 101	9:20 26
4:26-29 10	9:58 81
4:30-21 9	10:25-29 . . . . 103, 106
5:7 . . . . 31, 126	10:27 144
7:6 42	10:30-35 104–5
8:27-30 26	11:20 9
8:31 35	13:31-35 147–48
9:7 . . . . 31, 36, 45, 122, 126	15. 98
9:9 . . . . 126, 129	15:2 . . . . 97–98, 111
9:38 10	15:3-7 . . . . 97, 118
10:46 122	15:8-9 111
12:35-37 27	15:11-32 . . . . 89, 107–8, 111, 119
13:21-27 131	17:20-21 102
13:26 . . . . 33, 34	21:34-36 103
14:28 17	23. 149

23:24	149
23:39-43	150
23:46	149
23:47	149
24	19
24:13-15	19
24:34	149
24:46-47	150

John

1:1	8, 67
1:1-3	54
1:1-14	65–67, 153
1:6-9	67
1:10-11	67
1:14	20, 53, 68
1:20, 23	156
1:34	156
1:35-37	8
1:46-55	55
2:1-20	52
3:11-15	36
3:16	32
3:17-21	156
5:31	156
5:37	38, 157
6:63	154
6:67-69	154
8:17-18	157
9:35-38	36
10	151
10:1-6	20
11	14
14–17	151
14:13	32
15	151
15:26	157
15:27	157
17:1	32
18:4-6	155, 157–58
19:35	157
20:28	21, 28, 29
20:29	20
20:30-31	3, 26, 32, 158
21	16

Acts

2:1-36	148
7	149
9:1-22	16
10:22	144
10:43	150
11:26	24
13:16	144
13:26	144
13:33	130
13:38	150
20:17-35	148
22:1-16	16
26:9-18	11
26:18	150

Romans

1	31
1:1-4	23, 25
1:4	30
3:5	90–92
3:23	90
3:26	24
4:24	24
5:18-19	92
8:3	3
13, 14	83
14	83–90
14:1-9	84
14:4	90
14:7-9	85

1 Corinthians

1:3	28
1:3-4	41
4:8	87
6:15	94
8:1-13	85
8:6	73
11	120

11:23 24
11:29-30 44
12:2-13 .... 27, 92
12:3 28
14:9-2 93
15. .... 9, 17, 86, 100
15:3-7 15
15:4 15
15:8 .... 15, 88
15:12-27 .... 87, 88
15:22 89
15:28 90
15:32 87

2 Corinthians
4:14-15 82
8:1-14 .... 80–83, 84
8:9 .... 81, 82

Galatians
1:11-16 16
3:26-27 32
4:4-5 32

Ephesians
2:14 60

Philippians
2:6 .... 59, 70
2:6-7 60
2:6-11 62–63
2:9, 11 29

2:10 63
2:11 .... 27, 63, 89

Colossians
1:15 .... 60, 70
1:15-20 69–73
1:18 70
1:20 .... 70, 72

1 Thessalonians
1:1 24

Hebrews
2:5-6 34

1 John
4:9 32

2 John
1:3 32

Revelation
1:12-16 74
1:14-15 74
4:1 74
5:12 75
5:12-13 75
5:13 75
7:10, 12 74–75
11:15-18 74
15:3-4 74
21 74

www.ingramcontent.com/pod-product-compliance
Lightning Source LLC
Chambersburg PA
CBHW011747220426
43667CB00021B/2931